Birth Mother

Trauma

AMERICAN ADOPTION CONGRESS
1000 Connecticut Ave., N.W., Suite 9
Washington, D.C. 20036

A Counseling Guide

For Birth Mothers

By

Heather Carlini

Morning Side Publishing
1992

First printing: July 1992

Editor: Michelle West (Toronto)

Printed and bound in Canada by Scott Printing

Canadian Calaloging in Publication Data:

Carlini, Heather 1947

Birth Mother Trama

ISBN # 0-9696295-0-8

1.   Unmarried Mothers -- Counseling of.
2.   Birthparents -- Counseling of.

1. Title.

HV700.5.C37 1992   362.83'9286   C92-091603-1-

Acknowledgements

Thank you to Michelle West (Toronto), my brilliant editor, who recognized this book, pruned it, and encouraged me to dig deeper, so that I could really reach out to help birth mothers. Thanks to Charlene Lightfoot of the Adoption Connection, (my critique in Utah) whose encouragement and suggestions were certainly needed. Thanks to Jone Carlson of People Searching News, Florida, who gave numerous suggestions of which I tried to follow. Thanks to Wanda Pillon of Parent Finders B.C. who supplied me with needed information from time to time while doing my research. Thanks to Lorna Walker who proof read for me and nurtured my creativity.

A very special thanks to all the fine birth mothers who participated in my research by either filling out questionnaires or allowing me to interview them. Your names will remain anonymous to protect your idenities. Your contributions made this research all "fit together" to form the pages within. It will hopefully help other birth mothers who have yet to make the healing journey.

And last but not least, I want to thank my wonderful husband who shared the heartache over the years, and yet never gave up the hope that we would one day find our son. His belief in my ability to write this book was truely inspiring.

Also, a very special thanks to our daughter Michelle who's encouragement to write the book during the summer of 1991 was the "wind beneath my wings" when the going was tough!

The purpose in writing this book is to share with you, my readers, the results of six years of research into what I call "Birth Mother Trauma". This is the lingering affects leftover from having to relinquish a child to adoption. My intense interest in the subject stems from the fact that, I too, am a "birth mother". I have experienced a lot of what I write about in this book. In my research, I have tried to measure to what degree various birth mothers experienced suffering following the separation of the mother and child. I <u>realize</u> <u>that</u> <u>some</u> <u>women</u> <u>went</u> <u>on</u> <u>as</u> <u>if</u> <u>the</u> <u>matter</u> <u>didn't</u> <u>bother</u> <u>them;</u> <u>but,</u> <u>this</u> <u>book</u> <u>is</u> <u>for</u> <u>the</u> <u>women</u> <u>that</u> <u>it</u> <u>did</u> <u>bother</u>.

By profession, I am a Counselor and a Certified Graphologist, specializing in counseling women. My research was done from 1986 to 1992. I interviewed a total of 198 women from various parts of Canada and the U.S., plus 2 psychologists (1 male and 1 female). The women ranged in age from 27 to 68 with the median age being 41. They were either connected with adoption support groups, or they had placed ads in the newspapers looking for their children. I was very touched by the openness of the birth mothers who participated in my research. Finally someone cared about their feelings and they willingly opened up to help me as much as they could. I will forever be indebted to these fine women.

THE HISTORY OF ADOPTION IN NORTH AMERICA

Adoption laws, as we know them today in North America, had their beginning in the early 1920's. World War I produced many out-of-wedlock pregnancies to women who didn't receive the support of their families or government to facilitate keeping their babies with them. It was thought to be a "sin" to have a child "out of wedlock", so she was expected to give up the baby to a married couple who would supposedly provide a better life for the child than had she raised it on her own. The birth mother was often made to feel "bad" for wanting to keep her baby but, at the same time, wasn't offered any other alternatives.

Social workers, back then, felt that the only way the system could operate properly was to have the child never learn of their "sinful beginnings". Consequently, as a result of this way of thinking, many adoptees weren't told of their adoption, and in some cases, if they were told, the story was often a fabrication about the birth mother. Adoption, in this sense, was supposed to erase all blood lines with the biological family, and now this child was joined to the blood line of the adoptive family by name only, on a piece of paper.

Over the years, much of the old beliefs regarding adoption have fortunately changed, but the rationale for them still remains. There is a movement to try to change these archaic laws, to put more of a human element into the entire process, but we still have a long way to go before a proper system is established. At the present time, some adoption agencies are telling us that they have implemented the "open adoption" method. This method allows the birth mother to stay in the child's life, and the biological ties aren't completely severed. The agencies also say that proper counseling is given to the adoptive parents and the birth mother, in their joint efforts to raise the child. This method may be an improvement over adoptions of years ago; but, it will take another twenty years to find out if this system really works. **Note:** I must add here that the young "unwed" mother today has more alternatives than the women back in the 50's, 60's or even the 70's because society doesn't shame-base her into relinquishment. Usually the family will help or (even if they won't), most governments will assist the mother financially to help her keep her child. In many areas, the government will also assist her with day-care costs while she works, in order to support her child.

It is no wonder that there is such a need for counseling for both birth mothers and adoptees. Adoption agencies are beginning to see more and more of them show up at their doors searching for each other. These same agencies now admit that yesterday's system of doing adoption was quite inadequate when it came to the issue of how the birth mother was treated. However, they can't do much about it at this late date. They have their hands tied when it comes to helping those search- ing, since they have a binding contract with the adoptive parents. Instead, they now refer the adoptee and birth parents to the reunion registries It is easy to understand why the birth mother goes through so much anger and depression over the years. Closed adoption for her had the most dehum- anizing affect that you can imagine. Yesterday's birth mother was often treated horribly through the adoption process and now society is beginning to realize the injustice done to these women. In many cases, her family wouldn't discuss the issue with her any further, nor did the adoption agencies want anything more to do with her. She then began to set up a denial system within her psyche to accom- modate all the hidden pain.

VI OPENING

Not all birth mothers have suffered to the same degree of pain, nor do they react in the same way to suffering. Some are better at using denial than others, and may not think that the adoption issue still bothers them. If you are a birth mother, and you feel that you have recovered, I challenge you to read the book and discover what can actually happen to the birth mother over the years, and see if you relate to at least some of it. It may surprise you!

I set up the book to give you as much information as I could regarding the lingering psychological affects that plague many birth mothers for years following relinquishment. Also, it addresses the physical affects that can occur due to the buried emotions turning inward. I have tried to suggest methods of treatment that you can seek out from professionals, along with offering you a recovery program that should help many of you to rid yourself of some of the locked-up emotional baggage This is done in an effort to help you get back in touch with your real feelings once more. Nothing can ever take away all the sorrow of losing a child to adoption, but this book is meant to be a guide to help you cope with the pain while you possibly begin to see things in a different light. It is difficult for many birth mothers to resolve or close the issues related to adoption, so you see why it is important to go through a healing process. Each chapter in this book is meant to open up another part of the healing process, allowing you to finally move your life forward creating a renewing of the mind and spirit.

I suggest that you read through the book once, then slowly read it again, only this time, do the exercises in depth. Give yourself plenty of time to work on each one.

Note: in this book you will notice that I have a tendency to overuse certain terms such as: "many birth mothers", "some birth mothers", or "the birth mother". The reason for this is that I can't say that everything that I write about will apply to your case. I simply use these terms because they are facts that I uncovered in my research and there seems to be a trend that occurred among "many birth mothers". Also, if you find a bit of repeat in other areas of the. book, it is simply meant to keep you focused on the issues that we are working on. Please bear this in mind while reading!

Also, the book isn't meant to be a cure-all for every birth mother. Some of you may need more help than I can provide. I have written the book to bring the various issues to your attention so that you will know where to go for help and what kind best suits the birth mother. On the other hand, insight is empowering within itself to many of you.

Research

Everyone else has spoken for and about the birth mother, but my research went directly to the birth mother to listen to how she really feels.

The following questions are a cross–section of questions asked in the survey. The rest of the research is incorporated into the various chapters.

1.   What was the status of your relationship with the birth father at the time of the relinquishment?

76% a long term relationship
20% close friends
4% casual relationship

2.   What was your reason for relinquishing your baby?

38% unmarried and were given no support to keep their children.
53% pressured by a social worker or parents while being reminded of the stigma of being an unwed mother.   They were also told that the baby would be better off with a two–parent family.
9% told by a clergyman of their church that in order to be forgiven of her "sin", they would have to give up their babies.

Note: Not one of the birth mothers that I inter- viewed said that they didn't want their children. On the contrary –– they were made to feel that they had "no other choice".   At the time of the relin- quishment there was no government support for the single birth mother such as their is today.

3. Regarding the story that the adoption agency told you about the adoptive family: Was there any descrepency between the original story that you were told and the story that you may have been told years later in a non-identifying letter about the adoptive family (if you received one)?

87% reported that the story was different the second time around.

4. When you returned to the adoption agency in the last few years for additional or updated information about your son or daughter, how were you treated?

82% reported that the agency treated them with little regard for their intense feelings and they preferred not to deal with them. However, within the past ten years, most adoption agencies began steering the birth mother to the newly established reunion registries, instead of dealing with them themselves.

18% reported that the social workers were sympathethic, but apologized for not being able to give any identifying information (to help with her search). The women were given a letter with non-identifying information about the adoptive family instead.

Note: Some adoption agencies are now beginning to give the birth mother the first name of the adoptee when she shows up for information. This is sometimes helpful if you are in the midst of a search.

5.   Have you told your husband about the adoption?

89% reported yes
11% reported no

6.   What was your highest level of education obtained?

35% high school
65% further education (university or college)

7.   Do you feel that you suffered from an enormous amount of grief over the years due to losing your child?

ALL SAID "YES"

8.   Do you feel that you suffer from low self-esteem because of having to give up your child?

85% reported yes
15% reported that they tried to boost themselves up in other ways.

9.   Do you feel a sense of betrayal over having lost your child?

76% reported yes
24% reported no because they blamed themselves.

10. **Have you gone for counseling since relinquishing your child, or do you feel the need?**

32% received counseling
14% possibly in the future
54% undecided

11. **Have you ever suffered from any phobias?**

9% reported "yes" that they had suffered from
Claustrophobia, and some of these same women also
suffered from a slight case of Agoraphobia (at
some point over the years).

12. **When asked how many would search for their
child -- the answers were:**

23% had reunions already
64% said they planned to search
9% were in the midst of a search
4% were afraid of rejection, but may consider a
search in the future.

Most of these women stressed the fact that they
didn't want to upset the adoptive parents. They
respected them and their feelings.

Table Of Contents

-XII-

Birth Mother Trauma

The birth mother, in many cases, endured insurmountable pain and survived in spite of it. She is a woman whose life's circumstances were altered through the relinquishment of her child years ago. Along with possibly losing respect for herself, she sometimes loses respect for and trust in the people who encouraged her to relinquish her child against her will, rather than supporting her in her efforts to keep her baby. In the book, I refer to these people as her "significant others".

[handwritten margin note: the bias in this book is a tad heavy handed!]

Perhaps the most painful loss for the birth-mother was the loss of her dreams. As she looked at her baby in the hospital nursery, she had certain hopes for him or her. These hopes didn't include his or her being placed with another family. The dreams and promises for this tiny baby weren't spoken, but they were there; however, the birth mother had to endure the loss and disappoint-ment instead. She stood in the face of reality and had to put her feelings aside to accommodate the wishes of her "significant others". It was at this point that her hopes and dreams were crushed. This wasn't what she wanted, hoped for, asked for, or prayed for. The dream died and along with it a part of the mother went also, only to be awakened years later when the truth surfaces once more. This time she may begin to entertain the thought of finding her child in hopes that he or she will forgive her and understand what happened years ago.

[handwritten margin note: As a birth mother, mine would have include such hope.]

Back at the time of the relinquishment, the birth mother often felt that her feelings and wants were abandoned and disregarded. Now, years later, it is important that she has someone to help her validate those feelings of years ago and support her through the grief. Without allowing herself to go through this process, her life is frozen in some areas within the subconscious.

[handwritten margin note: I don't think that this author thinks she can decide what you thought/think. She perpetuates rather than corrects the tradition of ignoring birthmothers thoughts.]

2 UNFINISHED BUSINESS

For many women, mid-life crisis brings on issues of unfinished business from earlier years and the birthmother is no exception to the rule. In many cases she has a lot more unfinished business than other women.

Often, it is when the children leave home, a marriage goes sour or a parent dies that other things begin to "seep out" of the subconscious. It may be at this time that a woman begins to encounter mood changes, crying, restlessness, irritatility sleep or appetite changes, or loss of energy. This may be a "cathartic" period where she tries to understand the left-over feelings from years ago. Back when she was parted from her child, she had to put the event behind her and forget how she felt, and as a consequence of suppressing all those "special" feelings, now she sometimes has a difficult time identifying with what she actually feels inside. This can set up a system within her psyche that whenever she feels something special, she tries to avoid the feeling. Constant denial and avoidance of the adoption issue over the years may have the effect of making her chronically anxious whenever the issue surfaces. It is most likely that she isn't consciously aware of the cause of her anxiety. The kind of anxiety that we're talking about here is what surfaces when "trigger situations" begin to happen. These "trigger situations" are: seeing another child about the same age and gender as her relinquished child, her child's birthday, Christmas, Thanksgiving, Easter or any other time of the year when there is a family gathering. It is at times like these, that she becomes super aware that someone is missing from the picture.

It isn't unusual for birth mothers to lose touch with the emotional part of themselves. They develop a way of withdrawing emotionally to avoid being hurt any further. This is one reason that many birth mothers go for years without talking about the relinquishment. Hurt has been piled upon hurt and one day she becomes overloaded. She then begins to reject emotional honesty because she feels that talking about the event of so many years ago may cause shock in others. She may also have been so hard on herself over the issue, that someone else's ridicule may be difficult for her to handle.

Many times, she will try to make these intense feelings go away because she becomes frightened of them. To acknowledge just how she really feels would demand a decision (action or change) on her part which would open her up to reality. She would then become aware of her personal wants and needs and have to do something about them.

Part of the birth mother's recovery is to realize that her feelings from years ago are important. They count. The emotional part of her is special and she must try to rediscover this important part of herself once more.

The emotional part of her is the core of her existence -- it is the part that laughs and cries. It opens her up to giving and receiving love, making her feel closer to others. On the other hand, negative emotions about the past keep her from moving forward. Anger can turn into resentment and bitterness that threatens to linger indefinitely. Also, sadness about the relinquishment many times turns into chronic depression that seems inescapable.

4 WAKING UP THE FEELINGS

With practice and awareness, you (the birth mother) can awaken the emotional part of yourself. You need to invite emotions back into your life and make a commitment to stay in touch with your feelings from this point forward.

In the next few pages, we will begin to explore just how you were able to hide the pain over the years, how it begins to surface, and how you are going to heal all this by integrating the various feelings and emotions once more -- in order to feel whole.

Birth mothers often carry around excessive baggage in the form of rules from years ago (old rules, that don't really apply to today's world). These old rules now need to be reexamined because they are such a part of her psyche that they can cause her damage in the stage of today's present culture. The old rules focused more on what the "neighbors thought", or the "family honor", rather than on how the birth mother felt about herself. Rather than helping her to keep her baby, and be responsible, yesterday's rules taught her to hide the shame, and deny her feelings. They taught her a system of codependency, where the feelings and thoughts of others were more important than how she herself felt. Her life sometimes became filled with living up to everyone else's expectations, and at the same time, it was the beginning of a deep void within her own psyche. It was an emotional amputation of sorts.

Many birth mothers going through recovery have enormous difficulty discerning whether they, or someone else, was responsible for their problems. This is characteristic of women whose sense of self has been broken down due to the relinquishment of a baby. There is a tendency, however, for women who feel this way, to blame themselves for everything that happened years ago. In this case, she owned the blame for everyone else, including the biological father, and for her parents who didn't offer their support, along with owning her own blame. Society also blamed her for everything. This was the "blame the victim" syndrome,in which the birth mother internalized society's message of yesterday and blamed herself also. She felt that she caused all the heartache by being a "bad person" to whom bad things happened.

I truly believe that if these same women had been offered some support, and encouragement to keep their babies years ago, there wouldn't have been many adoptions at all. Thank goodness it is different today. Unwed mothers have plenty of support to keep their children, and government assistance is available to facilitate keeping the baby with the birth mother. Society has also taken on a kinder attitude towards such matters, and realizes that it is important for children to be with their biological mothers whenever possible. Statistics show that one in four children born today is to an unwed mother, and yet it is almost impossible to find children to adopt. This definitely tells us something.

In this chapter, we are going to discuss "Repressions", what they are and just how they affect the birth mother years after the relinquishment.

According to Freud, "repression" is one of a number of defense mechanisms by which the Ego (our Conscious Self) blocks off threatening thoughts or desires and keeps them from "seeping" into our conscious mind. When we repress thoughts in the subconscious mind, the ego uses up some of its own energy sources. The more painful the memory, the more energy the Ego must expend in order to keep the memory repressed.

Some birth mothers go into a prolonged mourning process when they feel suspended in the past (if only on a subconscious level). In many ways, they hang on to unremitting grief, clinging without relief to their sorrow, guilt, anger, self-hatred and depression. These then become your repressions. The avoidance of these painful feelings on a conscious level can be maintained sometimes for years or even a lifetime until you find a way to recover.

Since repressed feelings are blocked energy, they have the power to turn inward, causing headaches, stomach disorders, backaches or a general weakened physical condition. Some doctors believe that they actually have an affect on our immune system also. This in turn leaves the body open to all sorts of illnesses and diseases. So you can understand why it is important that you begin to release some of this negative energy -- otherwise, other areas of your life are disturbed.

Repressing feelings, especially if you are doing this in the Denial Stage of the grief process (this is when you are not yet aware that the relinquishment still affects you), can lead to compulsive behaviors such as overeating, overspending, smoking, drinking, taking drugs, etc. These repressed feelings have a way of eating at the core of your existence.   The longer you hold on to them, the more power they have over you.

In order to avoid these hurtful feelings locked within,many of us have learned a system of using defense mechanisms. As we already discussed,Repression is one of these.[We will discuss the others in the chapters to follow.]   Our feelings become blocked when we repress them. The only way we can handle these blocks is to acknowledge their presence, and to realize what defense mechanisms are being used to keep the system in a dysfunctional pattern.

Not all of you will have the same defense mechanisms to hide the hurtful memories, but you will surely recognize a couple that you have used. Please keep in mind that not all birth mothers carry the same amount of pain. I wrote the book to help you recognize the symptoms of "Birth Mother Trauma" so you can find a way to recover.

Part of the recovery process is gaining insight into the various problems that can occur when hurtful memories are repressed. Another part of the process involves doing exercises to let out the emotions that need to be expressed. You will need a notebook or looseleaf binder to keep a daily journal of your progress, and to do the exercises that I will be presenting to you. Do the exercises over the space of at least a month or longer, or until you have worked through the various issues.

To give you an example of just how birth mothers use " Repression" as a defense mechanism, let's examine just what happens when they go into "Delayed Grief".

Many birth mothers were expected to move forward and "forget what happened". So she would then try to go on without showing any emotion. She would never deny what happened, but she would begin to deny just how much it mattered to her and hurt her. This denial caused her to delay her grief until a later time in life. One of the reasons the birth mother goes into "Delayed Grief" is that there is usually nobody around to validate and support her through her pain. It is difficult to grieve alone, so many birth mothers suffered alone by crying into their pillows at night or locked behind a bathroom door. Many suffered from the "aching arms" syndrome in the middle of the night. I was surprised, when doing my interviews, to find out just how many birth mothers spoke of experiencing this because I did also.

"Delayed Grief" is the core of what is called "Post-Traumatic Stress Syndrome". Soldiers who have been to war will often suffer symptoms years later when something pulls the painful memories out of their subconscious. Some of the symptoms are: feeling out of control, feeling suspended in time, sleep disorders, eating disorders, panic attacks, anxiety and sometimes phobias. The reasons for the grief may be different, but many of the symptoms are also common to some birth mothers, as they also suffer from "Delayed Grief" in the same way.

Holding on to too many "repressions" can cause the birth mother a great deal of anxiety and, at some point, if the anxiety becomes too overwhelming, there is a chance that it can turn into various phobias. Many therapists feel that these phobias are defense structures within the psyche. The subconscious mind can hold just so many repressed feelings and, at some point, they may begin to surface as physical illnesses or as misunderstood fears. What may be happening here is that she becomes unable to deal with the repressed memories of the relinquishment inside her subconscious, and so she begins to project these feelings onto other people or objects. This is an attempt within her psyche to dispose of the bad memories, so she may begin to place the blame for her uneasiness on outside reasons. For a short time this brings her a sense of security and temporary relief from the original problem (the painful memories).

Please note the following if you suffer from phobias: Sometimes the original source of the pain is too overpowering for some birth mothers to handle on their own; therefore, it is advisable that you find some form of therapy to help you explore the shame and slowly begin to integrate the split-off experiences (phobias) with the original problem.

It is believed, by some psychologists, that if the birth mother hasn't handled the relinquishment issues before mid-life, then at this time she may begin to suffer from unexplained illnesses or phobias. This frequently happens to many birth mothers between the ages of thirty-five and forty-five. The reason for this is probably the mid-life crisis, when issues from the past begin to surface. The phobias are often "triggered" by a traumatic life event, such as the death of a parent, loss of a job, or a divorce, etc. The loss seems to have the effect of pulling out memories of the past from the subconscious.

Some of the birth mothers, that I interviewed, told me about developing Agoraphobia, (the fear of going outside the house). They spoke of feeling out of control, and this led many of them into panic attacks at the thought of having to do anything outside the house. Being locked within their home gives them a sense of physical boundaries that are very predictable. Being outside these boundaries gives them a fear of losing control. They explained it as operating out of fear, and some felt that the phobia had its beginning around the same time that some trauma happened in their lives. This trauma seemed to have the effect of pulling out memories from the past regarding the relinquishment of their baby. *None of them report-ted having a history of Agoraphobia in their family

There are many theories on treating Agora-phobia -- Psychotherapy (using Freudian techniques) which works with childhood memories; but, it doesn't seem to offer much insight or explanations regarding relinquishment issues. Another theory of Agoraphobia assumes that the symptoms are a result of a disease. In this treatment, the practitioner treats the symptoms with drugs. Supportive Therapy is also added to the treatment. One of the draw-backs in this treatment is that you can become phy-sically and psychologically addicted to the drugs (this therapy doesn't appear to offer much help with the relinquishment issues neither).   Still another treatment for this phobia is Behavioral Therapy, in which the therapist tries to desensitize the patient of his or her fear. This seems to work well with the simple phobias (such as the fear of crowds), but it still doesn't address the conflicts of the relinquishment.   [The birth mothers, that tried this treatment, reported that they didn't feel that it worked for them.]   One recent form of therapy is "Exposure Therapy", in which people are taught techniques for coping with anticipated anxiety and panics. This method of treatment seems to be more helpful for the birth mother, because it can incorporate dealing with relinquishment issues at the same time. An authority on this type of treatment is <u>Dr. Alan Goldstein,</u> the Director of the Agoraphobia and Anxiety Program at Temple University in Philadelphia. If you are suffering from Agoraphobia yourself, you may want to read his book called <u>Overcoming Agoraphobia</u> which is co-authored by Berry Stainback. Penquin Books is the publisher. <u>I believe that this book offers some of the best help that a book can offer.</u>   You may, also want to find, a therapist who uses this type of treatment in your own community.

For a current listing of programs in your area you may write to the following address:

The Phobia Society of America
133 Rollins Avenue, Suite 4B
Rockville, Maryland 20852-4004
Telephone Area Code 301 231-9350

Many birth mothers, will confess to feeling unloved or rejected in current relationships, not realizing that the roots of rejection are internal rather than external. Her life may be full of put-downs because she projects that others don't love her. The fact is,that probably she doesn't love herself, and she is projecting this onto others.

[In my interviews, I found that many birth mothers spoke of having a difficult time with intimacy; consequently, many had divorces.]

Part of her recovery is to learn to love herself and others more fully. Women are great at nurturing others, but somehow they find it difficult to love themselves. We will explore this in the following chapters.

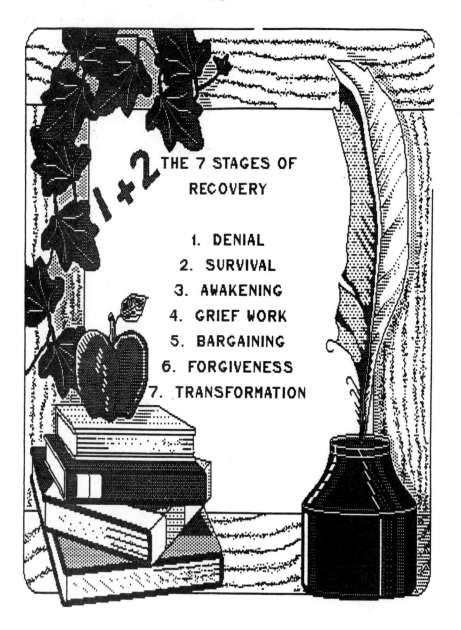

1 + 2

THE 7 STAGES OF
RECOVERY

1. DENIAL
2. SURVIVAL
3. AWAKENING
4. GRIEF WORK
5. BARGAINING
6. FORGIVENESS
7. TRANSFORMATION

In your recovery you will work through seven stages. The first one is the "Denial Stage". This stage began just after you were parted from your baby. You tried to do what everyone told you to do. Consequently, this was the beginning of an internal system within your psyche that denied your innermost feelings.

Let's discover just what this stage is about and how you can sometimes stay stuck in it.

Possibly, you may have felt that being an unwed mother years ago stereotyped you. And to admit that you had to relinquish a child to adoption may have made you feel a lot of self-hatred inside. You probably felt horrible about what had to be done, and yet you want to believe in yourself and who you are today. This causes ambivalence in many birth mothers.

Also, you may feel that if others find out your secret, they may think less of you because of it. Over the years, you may have been criticized for what you had to do, and you in turn criticized yourself. Experiences like this may have had the effect of making you feel that you have "no right" to feel anything special about the past.

There may be a fear that opening up the past may be too painful, and you may be afraid that if you were to admit just how much losing your child really meant to you -- then you might have to do something about it.

Thoughts that keep you locked in the Denial Stage are:

- it doesn't matter anymore
- I got over it a long time ago
- there's no need to think about the past anymore
- it was the best thing for everybody concerned

Many birth mother's become stuck in the Denial Stage. They enter it the day they had to relinquish their child and some of them stay stuck in this stage for years. Possibly, at the time of relinquishment, you were young and too hurt to fully comprehend the emotions that you were experiencing. You needed to protect yourself by pretending that you recovered, when you really didn't. You needed to fulfill everybody else's expectations by moving your life forward as if the event never occurred. With this in mind, you likely weren't completely aware of the full impact of what was actually happening, nor did you realize that others were also letting you down by not supporting you in your efforts to keep your baby. And the entire time you may have felt that you were letting everybody down by disappointing them. You felt confused and alone in a time of mixed emotions **No one was there validating those special feelings that you had back then --but now we are going to do just that.**

The Denial stage is familiar to the birth mother, and when you are used to operating out of this stage, it is hard to change. Many birth mothers will maintain that the event didn't really affect them, and they will have a tendency to intellectualize that the event was the best for everybody involved. **To deny the fact that you were hurt, at the time of the relinquishment, only serves to deceive yourself and keep you locked in Denial.**

To say that the matter no longer affects you and that you survived it, and forgot about it, keeps you from realizing the problems that you may be having today are a result of yesterday's problems. You may feel that you don't need to go through a recovery program because you have already healed. When you are doing this, you are running the risk that the denial can turn inward causing more repressions in the subconscious (such as we discussed in chapter 2).

Too many repressions (repressed memories) in the subconscious have a way of ruining other areas of our life in the present. For instance, when you lose touch with your feelings from the past, it is also difficult to recognize your feelings in the present. There is no peace of mind or contentment when this happens. It takes a lot of energy to repress feelings, and this is what I refer to as "negative energy", because it is destructive to you.

Not only does it take excessive energy to stay in the Denial Stage, but sometimes birth mothers will use mind-altering substances to keep them from feeling the feelings. These substances may be in the form of alcohol, tranquilizers,antidepressants etc. Others will take on compulsive behaviors such as over-eating, bulimia, excessive smoking, workaholism, excessive shopping, excessive cleaning etc. These are ways to divert the pain, but it is possible that the birth mother doesn't realize, on a conscious level, what it really driving her to be compulsive or to mind-alter. As you can see, the problem has multiplied because now there are addictions to handle.

The second stage of recovery is "Survival". To arrive at this stage of recovery, you had to survive the relinquishment. Over the years, you may have used many coping skills and ego defenses to do this. You learned how to deny, adapt, and survive.

When the birth mother has to give up her child against her will, she sometimes has a fracture occur in her personality. This fracture occurs when the "True Self" that she once was, at the time of relinquishment, becomes buried in shame, remorse and sadness in the subconscious, where it is disowned and forgotten temporarily. She may begin to reject this part of her personality because there was no one to validate those special feelings for her baby years ago, so she begins to ignore those feelings herself. She begins to shut down that part of her psyche and treats it harshly. For means of clarification, let's call this side of the personality the "Forgotten Self". Now she has to create an exterior side of the personality to pretend that the hurt doesn't exist or, in other words, to hide the shame -- this side of the personality we will call the "False Self". **(Remember, this isn't two personalities, it is just a fracture in your original personality -- your "True Self".**

The "False Self" was created by many birth mothers to accommodate the pain. She needed a new part that could pretend that she was doing fine, when she really wasn't. In order to keep the facade going, she would have to use new coping skills in order to survive all the pain. WE will now explore what these coping skills were and how they operated.

The Fracture

The "False Self" uses many <u>defense</u> <u>mechanisms</u> to protect itself from being traumatized. These defense mechanisms have three characteristics in common:

They are ways of trying to reduce the stress.

They deny and distort reality.

They operate on a subconscious level.

Before you can give up these defense mechanisms, it is important to explore what they are and how you use them.

The most common defense mechanisms used by birth mothers are:

<u>REPRESSION</u> - this is where the "False Self" stops threatening thoughts or desires from being conscious.

<u>DENIAL</u> - this is where you shut part of your memories off from reality.

<u>PROJECTION</u> - feeling that others will dislike you if they find out about the past.

<u>DISPLACEMENT</u> - some birth mothers were so upset at having to give up their babies, that they began to dislike babies in general (for a short period of time).

<u>AVOIDANCE</u> - this is where you avoid talking about the relinquishment to avoid hurting.

RATIONALIZATION - the birth mother gives elaborate justification or apology for what she had to do.

SUBLIMATION - some birth mothers decided to become career women, or to fill their lives in some other way, rather than ever again wanting to be a mother. This is a form of self-punishment for many.

INTELLECTUALIZATION - this is where the birth mother tries to convince herself and others that giving up her baby was the best thing that she could do for him or her. She gives unnecessary explanation for her actions, even when she knew it wasn't true (or in other words, she was saying what she thought people wanted to hear).

PASSIVE-AGGRESSIVE BEHAVIOR - this is where the birth mother doesn't stand up for her rights, and puts the rights of others first (passive), or she comes on overly strong to establish her anger regarding relinquishment (aggressive).

These defense mechanisms serve to keep the system in balance, even if it is only on a dysfunctional level. It is important, in recovery, that you give up the "False Self" because it is the role that keeps the "True Self" frozen and hidden away in the subconscious. This role helped you to hide all the pain. It provided structure and definition and it prescribed its own set of behaviors and emotions. The "False Self" had the role of enabling you to hide the shame for the rest of the family.

Stage 3 "Awakening"

Awakening means to begin to look inside and acknowledge the intense pain that you have been enduring over the years. <u>Psychologists</u> tell us that sometimes we repress thoughts so deeply that we lose track of when, and how the pain actually started. However, I have yet to meet a birth mother that wasn't aware of the exact moment the original pain began. That day is etched in her brain forever.

When you begin to "awaken" this sleeping part of your subconscious, you will begin to go through what counselors call a "catharsis". This is when the feelings begin to come out of the subconscious. These feelings may be any of the following: anger, sorrow, resentment, self-hatred, remorse, shame and in the end love and acceptance. The awakening of these feelings is an indication that you are beginning to feel again, and are beginning to find your "True Self" that may have been buried deep within for years. For some it may be surprising at first, and there may be a tendency to want to shut down and repress these feelings once more. Whatever you do, hang in there --because on the other side of pain is happiness. <u>Look at this stage as a time of emotional and spiritual growth. It is a time of total awareness and the beginning of finding freedom from the pain. If you feel that you need added help in this stage, then by all means find a counselor who is trained to help you.</u>

It is a good idea to find an adoption support group to join, in your area, because they can offer you plenty of support. There are other birth mothers who have gone through this stage and they can be a wonderful source of support. When you reach this point in recovery, just talking to someone about the past and having your feelings recognized as being real, lifts a huge burden off your shoulders. You may be surprised at first, that you aren't the only birth mother that has suffered the same pain of relinquishment.

When you begin to move the process forward, you begin to move out of denial and into awareness. In this stage you begin to make nondenial statements such as:

..... the past still hurts me.
...... I have suffered long enough.
...... losing my baby really did hurt me.
...... I really need to find my child.

These statements affirm the fact that you really did suffer and relinquishing your child did have a major affect on your life. When you reach this point in recovery, you have just taken a giant step. As you begin to go into this stage, you may have a tendency to want to back up into the denial stage once more. This place (in your mind) was familiar to you and now you don't quite know what to expect when you move forward. However, once you experience the feelings, and start to release the emotions you will begin to feel some relief. With your new insight, you should begin to understand just how destructive the denial stage was , and you will be relieved to be moving forward.

As we already discovered, once you begin to open up and talk during the "Awakening Stage" of your recovery, many feelings begin to come out of the subconscious. Now, it is important that you let yourself experience these feelings as they occur, as this is part of the healing process.

Remember, allowing yourself to feel the anger is an important part of the grief-work, and you will probably find that this will be one of the strongest feelings to surface. The anger from not wanting to relinquish your baby has multiplied over the years and it served to cover up the hurt, pain and guilt. It is justified! It may be powerful to stay locked up in anger because it is a protective shield, but believe me, it is more productive to let go of it.

Repressed anger causes problems as it "leaks out" inappropriately at the wrong things (such as kicking the dog). At times like this, it becomes displaced anger. It keeps us from enjoying intimate relationships. Too much hidden anger in your subconscious causes bitterness and hatred, so you can see why it is important to get rid of it.

The main goal in recovery is to develop your own sense of psychological and emotional power so that you can live your life as fully as possible.

Many birth mothers felt powerless over the situation at the time of relinquishment because they weren't taken seriously as an individual. They felt all the anger inside, even though many women find the idea of anger unthinkable, no matter how justified. Women in general are taught to hide or suppress anger, and due to this, some birth mothers feel alarmed when they go through the awakening process and the anger begins to surface.

It is easier to rationalize that the anger is not justified. It is also easier to ignore it, hold it inside, bury it, displace it on other things such as scrubbing walls, or turning it inward and hating yourself.

Depression is the result of blocking feelings of anger, caused by feeling powerless over yourself and others. It becomes a vicious cycle that can be never ending without a recovery program.

When we talk about going through recovery in this book, we are talking about unblocking the emotional energy. You first have to identify feelings of anger and rage in yourself and then admit to them. The source of conflict must be examined, and in the birth mother's case, it is the relinquishment of her baby. You must release the anger in safe circumstances, such as the exercises that I have provide for you in the following pages. The next step is to recognize your right to feel anger, and to discover the power to deal both with it and its cause.

Since women are conditioned to suppress anger, it is believed, to express anger is to "act out" or to be "out of control". Now you must give yourself permission to "be angry". When you are accustomed to operating out of a safe place in your mind, it takes courage to want to move forward. You can now permit yourself to release the anger in safe circumstances -- so that you can constructively work through the problem.

As the anger is released, you will be surprised that expressing it won't destroy you. You will also be surprised to see that it doesn't have quite the power that you thought it had. Once this negative energy is released, you will begin to feel a degree of empowerment inside, and this is the beginning of opening up the healing process.

It builds on your self-esteem because now the anger is channeled outward instead of inward.

It gives you a sense of empowerment because now you are regaining your own personal sense of power.

It allows you to finally pay attention to your own natural instincts of love, while it helps you to drop the self-hatred.

It allows you to begin the forgiveness process with yourself and with your "significant others" from the time of the relinquishment.

It helps you to let go of the guilt, shame, embarrassment and humiliation that you held inside for so long.

It moves you out of the victim stage.

It allows the outward flow of emotional tension that enables you to feel more relaxed both mentally and physically.

Stage 4 "Grief Work"

In order for you to progress through the recovery stages, you must go through some grief work to acknowledge exactly what feelings were ignored in the past.

VALIDATION:

Before this grief can be resolved, several factors must be present. One is validation. The trauma over losing your child must be finally validated as being real before it can be resolved. Up to this point, you may possibly not be aware of the extent of your depression or anger, which is locked away in your subconscious, because you have never give yourself permission to "feel" the full impact of your grief. The very defenses that helped you survive the relinquishment trauma -- denial, repression, avoidance, displacement, projection, rationalization, sublimation, intellectualization, and passive-aggressive behavior now become barriers to your growth.

SUPPORT:

Another factor that must be present in order to resolve the grief is a strong support system. This can take the form of an adoption support group, a close friend, another birth mother who understands birth mother issues or a counselor. This allows you to "mirror off" someone and finally legitimize your feelings. The support isn't there to place blame on you. This is one of the issues that you may be struggling with -- self-blame and humiliation.

As you enter the "Awakening Stage" of recovery, you start to notice that feelings from the past begin to enter into your conscious awareness. It may have surprised you at first, but this is completely normal. It isn't anything to be alarmed about or afraid of -- it is just awareness and it is part of the recovery process. If you feel a bit of depression in this stage, remember this is where denial may become your defense mechanism to drown out your feelings once more. You may be thinking something like: "It was all my fault - I was a bad person and I deserved it". But was it really all your fault??? No, definitely not! You carried all the blame, and even victimized yourself in the process (along with being victimized by others) and this possibly caused you a deep emotional wound within your psyche. **You have to now realize that this wound was real in order to begin to validate and legitimize it.**

ANGER:

Once you validate the emotional wound of having been abandoned in your time of need by those you probably loved the most, there comes a point of anger. It is okay to allow yourself to feel this anger towards those who let you down by not supporting your in your efforts to keep your baby.

SADNESS AND HURT:

When you begin to realize that you were (possibly) betrayed, you may feel sadness and hurt feelings inside. It is very important to grieve the loss of your dream to keep your baby and it is important that you finally acknowledge this fact.

REMORSE:

The sadness and hurt are usually followed by remorse over having to give up your baby.

SHAME AND SELF-HATRED:

You carried the shame for everyone. This made you feel horrible inside and possibly set up a system of self-hatred. Through all this shame and abandonment, it is likely that you were left in absolute loneliness.

THE GRIEF WORK PROCESS:

In the following pages, I want to take you through the process of grief work. Even though it has probably been many years since the event hap- pened, the grief is sometimes still there (on a subconscious level) and, I believe, that it is im- portant to go through this process in order to heal. It takes time and effort , but the rewards make it all worth while.

I will describe the process and then I will take you through it -- I can't promise you just how long it will take as everyone is different -- but you will know yourself when you reach the end.

In this stage of recovery, you begin to discover the deep internalized shame about the relinquishment and begin to externalize it.   Through the process you:

1. Transform the shame of the relinquishment back into a set of feelings (i.e. sadness, anger, remorse, self-hatred, resentment etc.)

2. Reduce the shame of the relinquishment by understanding the issues that precipitated the giving up of you baby for adoption.

3. Give the shame back to the shameless signifigant others that made you go through the pain (if this was the case).

4. Begin to transform the blocked energy of the shame into "positive healing energy" as you begin to change your focus from the past to the present.

1.   The first objective is to transform the shame back into a set of feelings. In order to accomplish this we use the exercises provided in the following chapter. Through these exercises you will begin to gain some new insight into how you really felt years ago, and how these "hidden feelings" ruled different aspects of your life in the years that followed.

2.   The second objective is to begin to reduce the shame by understanding the issues that precipitated the relinquishment of your child. In this process, you stop blaming yourself fully and you begin to realize that all the "blame" didn't have to be totally owned by you.   Times were different years ago, and it surely wasn't your fault that you weren't offered the love and support that you so desperately needed to keep your baby. In the past, most young mothers weren't given a choice of what to do, so they did the only thing they could. They had to listen to their "significant others" because they were at their mercy.

3.   The third objective is to let go of the anger and self-hatred that you held inside for so long. You can now turn it around to where you are allowed to feel angry at others for having put you through the adoption (if this is your case). It may have been your parents, boyfriend, or an adoption agency who talked you into relinquishing your child. Years ago, many young women simply went in for counseling and the adoption agency would talk them into signing her baby away. She was vulnerable and they worked on her guilt. We will use letter-writing and transference exercises to let out the emotions in this case.

4. The fourth objective is to <u>release</u> the <u>emotions</u> <u>that</u> <u>have</u> <u>been</u> <u>locked</u> <u>in</u> <u>the</u> <u>subconscious</u> <u>for</u> <u>years.</u> We use script therapy, sentence-completion exercises, transference, meditation exercises and letter-writing exercises. This transforms the blocked emotional energy that is shame-based back into "positive healing energy".

Through the entire process of grief work, we go back and attempt to realize the original pain that occurred as a result of the relinquishment. In this process, you allow yourself to feel the emotions that you denied yourself years ago. Remember that the relinquishment included neglect of your emotional needs that were essential at that time. <u>Once</u> <u>these</u> <u>emotions</u> <u>are</u> <u>released</u> <u>you</u> <u>should</u> <u>begin</u> <u>to</u> <u>feel</u> <u>a</u> <u>renewed</u> <u>sense</u> <u>of</u> <u>self.</u>

Think of your mind as a computer. You already know that you have a conscious mind and a subconscious mind. Most of us use our conscious mind only 10% of the time; however, our subconscious mind controls us 90% of the time. It controls us through self-hatred, anger, remorse, resentment, hurt, shame and guilt. You now want to rid yourself of this excessive baggage -- so think of recovery as deleting some of the information on your hard drive. Once it is emptied, you then have more room to reprogram it with good stuff!

Let Go Of The
Emotional Baggage!

There's no doubt about it, the birth mother is a complex person. She may appear on the inside to be a competent person who is quite successful in her job and in her home life. She may be the ideal mother and wife. However on the inside the picture is sometimes far different. This same woman is often still dealing with the core issues left over from losing her baby. The issues in regards to relinquishment are the conflicts and problems that she endured over the years. These issues are often on both a conscious and subconscious level. They are as follows:

1. LOW SELF-ESTEEM:

Having never completely recovered from the shame of having to give up a baby, plus the ridicule (sometimes) offered to her from others, she often has a difficult time with her self-esteem.

As you progress through your recovery program and you begin to heal the old hurt inside, you should begin to feel a renewed interest in life, and you will begin to allow yourself to care more about yourself and others.

2. GRIEVING THE LOSS OF YOUR CHILD:

Many times it is harder to handle the loss of a child to relinquishment than to death, because the birth mother doesn't permit herself to grieve properly. She was expected to go on as if nothing happened, so the grief became blocked in the subconscious for years.

By the time you finish doing the exercises, you will have gone through the grief process and the grief will be freed from the subconscious as you bring it out into conscious awareness.

3. FORGIVING YOURSELF AND OTHERS:

This is a hard step, because it means that you begin to forgive yourself and those who convinced you to give up your baby. Betrayal is difficult to forgive.

Forgiveness is such a huge step that it will take its own recovery step. Forgiveness in this case, involves changing your focus from the past to the present and refusing to replay the hurtful memories constantly in your head.

4. BEING OUT OF TOUCH WITH YOUR FEELINGS:

You learn in recovery that you were out of touch with many feelings from the past, and as you proceed through the recovery steps you begin to get in touch with those feelings once more.

5. DIFFICULTY GIVING AND RECEIVING LOVE:

When you lose touch with your feelings , it is hard to feel emotions, so in turn you lose touch with your natural instincts also.

As you begin to get back in touch with your feelings from the past and present, you will begin to open up your natural instincts. It may seem strange but, once you get rid of all the emotional baggage within, then the one emotion that seems to come rushing on strongly is ---LOVE!!!

6. CODEPENDENCY:

Because birth mothers need so much compassion themselves, they sometimes tend to overdo it when it comes to giving compassion to others. Many of them learned a system of putting everyone elses feelings ahead of their own, to avoid taking care of their own needs.

In recovery, you learn to give as much attention to yourself as you do to others. There is no need to avoid your own needs and wants any longer.

7. SELF-HATRED:

This self-hatred is usually on a subconscious level and it stems from the lack of self-esteem and dislike for yourself for what you had to do years ago. As you go through recovery, your self-esteem begins to increase, and you drop the need for self-hatred.

8. DYSFUNCTIONAL SEXUAL PROBLEMS:

Some birth mothers still relate sex to the pregnancy that led to their giving up the baby, and this causes some of them to become sexually dysfuntional. This is another form of self-punishment,and it also stems from not being in touch with their natural instincts.

Here again, as you work on getting in touch with your feelings, and you begin to take on more compassion for yourself, you will also begin to get in touch with your natural instincts again.

These core issues present themselves as problems in everyday living for the birth mother for years after the relinquishment. In order for you to get to the root of these core issues, you must begin to get in touch with your feelings once more. This is done by learning to monitor your feelings (while doing the exercises provided), as you go through the recovery process, and learning to acknowledge what core issues are being involved.

We discussed in chapter four how the "True Self" sometimes turns inward and becomes the" Forgotten Self" at the time of the relinquishment.This part of the personality carried the pain, embarrassment and humiliation. The birth mother often rejects this part of her personality, and hides it away ,until she goes through a healing process to integrate the   two sides of the personality once more.

When you begin to understand that the situation was out of your control, and when you realize that there was no one offering you sympathy or support, then you can finally begin to forgive this part of yourself.

Once this part of you is recognized, accepted and loved, you can then integrate this part of the personality with the rest of the personality. This part, once integrated, can be a source of spontaneity, love and acceptance.

Before you can integrate this "Forgotten Self" so that it can exist in a harmonious relationship with the rest of you, you must first make contact with it in your subconscious, where this part of your personality resides. We do this by doing the five exercises that I have provided.

In my work as a Counselor and a Certified Graphologist, I often use an exercise called Script Therapy. In this exercise you use your dominant hand to ask questions of your "Forgotten Self". You then use your nondominant hand to write the answers. This brings the right hemisphere of the brain into action. It is thought, by brain researchers, that this area of the brain contains a vast untapped potential. It is also believed that writing with your nondominant hand is a direct channel to this potential.

Many therapists feel that the dominant hand works with the left side of the brain. This is the hemisphere connected with motor ability, dexterity, intellect, conscious awareness, etc. The right hemisphere works with our intuition, the subconscious, emotions, feelings, spontaneity and creativity.

As you learn to work with this technique, you will notice that the nondominant hand expresses the feelings and emotions that have been locked away for so long. It does so in a controlled, safe manner were they can be acknowledged and validated as being real. For many, the release of these emotions brings with it incessant relief, both physically and mentally as it helps to reduce the emotional baggage.

This exercise is very important for integrating the two sides of the personality. I use this exercise extensively and find it to be of considerable help to my clients.

You can open up the subconscious by writing with your nondominant hand -- just allow it to feely express the feelings. Try not to control what needs to be said and respect it for telling the truth. Allow it to express its reality.

Copy the questions at the end of this section into your loose-leaf binder with your dominant hand, and use your nondominant hand to write the answers. Allow at least a full page for each question and answer. Sometimes the answers will be long and other times they will be short. Don't push it -- allow yourself to be spontaneous. The writing may be messy, but the appearance isn't important. It is the message that we are concerned with here. Remember, the nondominant hand is the "Forgotten Self", and the purpose of this exercise is to finally recognize this part of the personality and begin to own it once more. Be sure to date your work for future reference.

It is best to pick   a time of day when you won't be   interrupted to do this exercise, as it takes quite a bit of concentration. I also suggest that you have a picture of yourself around the time you were parted from your baby (within a year or two is fine).

Close your eyes and imagine   yourself sitting on a bench with this young girl (your "Forgotten Self"). Tell her that you love her and embrace her in your mind before you ask her to open up and talk about her innermost feelings. Ask her the following questions:

1.   Who are you?

2.   What part of your deepest feelings, in regards to the relinquishment, do you wish to talk about today?

3.   What can I do to make you feel better today?

4.   How can I change things in the future?

Script Therapy

Dear Forgotten Self: I want you to know
that I'm here for you. What
would you like to tell me?
I want you to pay attention
to the feelings down inside.
Many times I feel smothered
and disowned. I need
to open up and feel
again. I need to feel needed

and valued left alone. I
will not to be to open up
and feel. -42-

Another method of integrating the two sides of the personality is to use sentence-completion exercises.   This is another powerful tool to awaken the subconscious, where the "Forgotten Self" resides.

A tape recorder can be used for doing the following exercise, or you can have a friend read you the sentence beginnings, and then   you write the endings.

Here again,   it is best to pick a time of day when you won't be interrupted, as it takes quite a bit of concentration.   I also suggest that you use the same picture of yourself, as in the other exercise,   to help you focus on your younger self. The next step is to close your eyes and imagine yourself sitting on a bench with this young person (your "Forgotten Self").   Tell her that you love her, and embrace her in your mind before you ask her to open up and talk about her feelings.

Each time you do this exercise you generate new endings that take you deeper and deeper into the psyche, giving you new insights and integraation. Be sure to date your work, and keep it. In order to facilitate spontaneity, it is best not to check the previous day's exercise before doing a new set.

USE ONLY YOUR DOMINANT HAND FOR THIS EXERCISE

Sentence-Completion Exercises

If the Forgotten Self in me could speak
she would say ...

I suspect that I am acting out of my
Forgotten Self when I ...

Sometimes the hard thing about accepting
my Forgotten Self is ...

If I were more forgiving of my Forgotten
Self I would ...

I would be more understanding of my
Forgotten Self if I ...

If I fully accept the Forgotten Self as a
valuable part of me, I would...

I would be kinder to my Forgotten Self if
I were to...

I am beginning to realize (about myself)...

When I look at myself from this point of
view, I want to...

Examples of how the "Forgotten Self" often feels:

1. If the "Forgotten Self" in me could speak, she would say ....

    .. I feel sad because my feelings don't count
    .. I feel angry when I have to hide my true feelings.
    .. I feel lonely and disowned.
    .. I feel abandoned and shamed.

2. I suspect I am acting out of my "Forgotten Self" when I ....

    .. want to be alone and feel sad.
    .. need someone to listen to how I feel about losing my baby.

3. I would be more forgiving of my "Forgotten Self" if I ....

    .. went to a support group and shared my story
    .. did the exercises in this book to acknowledge to what extent the relinquishment bothered me.

4. I would be kinder to my "Forgotten Self" if I were to ....

    .. stop the negative self-talk about myself.
    .. if I learned the art of self-nuturance and practiced it.
    .. if I refused to replay the old tapes in my head about how much I really did suffer years ago.

This is another powerful exercise, that can be used to integrate the personality. It is good to have a friend to take you through this exercise, so you don't lose your concentration. Have her write the answers in your loose-leaf binder, date it and save it for future reference. Some people like to use a tape recorder for this exercise and then they record their insights in their binder.

To begin this exercise, either lie in a comfortable position, or sit in a comfortable chair with your feet up. Make sure that thee won't be any interruptions. When you are completely relaxed, you are ready to begin.

Spend a few moments feeling relaxed, and just focus on your breathing. Breath deeper, and try to remove any distracting thoughts from your mind. When you are completely relaxed, you should be in what we call the Alpha brain wave state. This is the brain wave state that you are in just before going to sleep.

Be sure to write down in your loose-leaf binder any feelings that surfaced during this exercise.   Remember to allow yourself to feel these feelings as you experience them, and allow yourself to release the blocked emotional energy (through tears) as this is the entire purpose of the exercise.   Also, be sure to keep track of any new insights you learn in the session.

Practice this meditation exercise everyday for a month, or longer if needed, until the trunk is emptied. When you reach this point, you will then ask your "Forgotten Self" to join you as you descend the steps to reality. This will be your point of integration.

Now that you are completely relaxed, and breathing deeply, begin to imagine yourself in a room with a flight of steps leading up to a white door with brass fixtures. You are going to go up these steps in your imagination, and enter this door. Begin to climb, counting the steps 1..2..3..4..5..6..7..8..9..10.

You are now at the top of the stairs, and the door is in front of you .. reach for the door knob and turn it slowly until the door is open .. On the other side of the door you see your Forgotten Self in the form of your younger self..Look deeply into her eyes, and see the pain and loneliness that she is feeling deep inside her .. Embrace her and tell her that you care about her feelings, and that you are there to discover exactly what it is that she needs to tell you .. Notice that she has an old trunk sitting on the floor beside her .. In this trunk resides all the wisdom and hurt feelings that she wishes to share with you.....

Ask her if she would like to show you the gems of wisdom that the trunk holds .. she may be hesitant at first, but remind her that you love her and she can be healed with her cooperation .. Ask her what she wants you to do to heal these hurts, and promise her that you will do your best to take care of all these needs, from this day forward.

As you listen to what she has to say, allow yourself to recognize the feelings that she is awakening inside you .. <u>Take time to feel these feelings and savor the moment .. don't rush the process</u> ..

Before ending this session,be sure to embrace your Forgotten Self and thank her. Tell her that you are here for her, anytime she needs you, and you will never neglect her again.

Now go back down the steps until you reach the bottom 10..9..8..7..6..5..4..3..2..1 You have now reached the bottom of the steps and you feel completely awake and relaxed.

Transference Exercise

This is an exercise that you can do with a supportive person who understands the adoption issues. This person can play the role of someone that you are angry with --someone from the time of the relinquishment. This supportive person is supposed to guide you through the process without showing anger. It is important for you to get your deepest emotions out. **If you feel rage, experience it!!!** **If you feel anger, cry and get the emotions out!! GO WITH YOUR FEELINGS.**

Have your friend sit in a chair opposite you. Tell her the name of the person whose role you want her to play -- i.e. if this person was your mother --tell her "Mother, this is how I feel about what you had me go through years ago...and because of having to go through it I am still feeling...

Continue to go through all the roles of the people who upset you years ago, at the time of the relinquishment, and let the emotions flow freely.

Once the session is finished, be sure to keep a record of the feelings and insights that you experienced and date it.

This is an excellent exercise for getting out the angry feelings and lessening the emotional baggage inside your mind.

Another exercise that can be of benefit to some birth mothers is -- letter writing. The letter can be written to a "significant other" from the time of the relinquishment. In this letter you let out all the anger, resentment, guilt, remorse, or feelings of betrayal.

You may want to give this letter to the person, but probably the best idea is to just <u>let out the feelings and burn the letter</u>. <u>This is a symbolic way of ridding yourself of the hurtful feelings, and finally destroying them.</u> It is also a good way of getting rid of anger in a controlled manner.

CONFRONTING YOUR SIGNIFICANT OTHERS FROM THE TIME OF RELINQUISHMENT (These are the people who didn't support you in your efforts to keep your baby. They possibly upset you, made you angry, or just simply -- let you down!)

This format can be used for doing either your letter-writing exercises or your transference exercises.

1. List, or address exactly what this significant other did to upset you, let you down, shame-base you, or who simply just didn't support you in your efforts to keep your baby.

Examples:

- you made me feel as if my feelings didn't count.
- you ridiculed me for becoming pregnant without realizing that my baby was an impor-tant part of me.
- you controlled me, and didn't allow me to be part of the decision-making process regard-ing my baby.

2. List how you felt as a result of this person's insensitivity to your feelings.

Examples:

- I felt devalued as a person and unloved.
- I believed that I was "damaged goods".
- I was upset at you for not treating me like a person.

3. List what consequences the significant other's actions have on you in the present, and how your life is still affected.

Examples:

- it caused me to devalue my self-worth
- it has caused me to be compulsive about ---
- it has caused me to lose touch with my feelings, and my instincts.
- it caused me to be codependent -- putting the wants of others ahead of my own.

4. List or address what you would want from this person from here on.

Examples:

- I want you to listen to my true feelings from years ago, and how my baby meant so much to me.
- I want you to listen to my feelings about finding my child today.
- I never want to hear you ridicule me again regarding the relinquishment issue.
- I want you to own your part of the blame for not helping me to keep my baby, when it meant so much to me.

Positive Ways of Releasing Anger

Clean out your closets of old things left over from the past -- this has the same affect as cleaning out the mind.

Write letters to those that you are angry at (from the past) and burn them (the letters that is).

Do aroubics or running to bring on a feeling of well-being.

Use your Transference Exercises.

Use your Script Therapy Exercises.

Scrub the floors or walls.

Have a good cry.

Talk to a counselor or therapist.

Talk to someone in your support group.

Punch a pillow.

In chapter 4 you discovered how the birth mother often takes on an outer personality that we called the "False Self", in order to allow herself to survive the pain. It is, in essence, her facade. You discovered exactly how it operated, but now it is time to explore methods of giving up the role in order to integrate the fractured sides of the personality -- so they can become the "True Self" once more.

You discovered how the "False Self" used many defense mechanisms to protect itself from being traumatized. Now we will go on to discover how you can give up these defense mechanisms in order to make your life more functional. Remember -- not all birth mothers used them; but, many of you have used at least a couple.

In order to get rid of these defense mechanisms, we need to explore each one again.

1. **REPRESSION** -- You will recall the "False Self" would stop threatening thoughts or desires from entering your conscious mind --once you have worked on ridding yourself of the hidden emotions, then there will be no need to repress memories again.

2. **DENIAL** -- this is where you shut part of your memories off from reality. Here again, once you have gone through the Awakening Stage of recovery, then you are out of denial and you have acknowledged the memories as being real -- now they re-enter your reality.

3. <u>PROJECTION</u> -- Feeling that you are not loved because you don't deserve it. You should now begin to give up this defense mechanism as you begin to have more self-confidence and self-worth.

4. <u>DISPLACEMENT</u> -- Some birth mothers were so upset at having to give up their babies that they began to dislike babies in general for a short time. As you go through recovery you begin to get in touch with your feelings and instincts once more, and you will probably automatically give up this defense mechanism.

5. <u>AVOIDANCE</u> -- This is where you avoided talking about the relinquishment to avoid hurting. Now you have brought the issue out into the open so there is no need to avoid it any longer.

6. <u>RATIONALIZATION</u> -- You may have given elaborate justification or apology for what you had to do years ago, to appease everyone. Now you don't have to rationalize anything -- it happened and you handled it the best way you could.

7. <u>SUBLIMATION</u> -- Some birth mothers decided to become career women, or to fill their lives in some other way, rather than ever again wanting to be mothers. This was a form of self-punishment and it is no longer necessary to punish yourself any further.

8. <u>INTELLECTUALIZATION</u> --This is where the birth mother tries to convince herself and others that giving it up was the best thing that she could do for her baby. You don't have to convince anyone of anything now because this was a form of denial, in many cases.

9. PASSIVE-AGGRESSIVE BEHAVIOR - This is where the birth mother doesn't stand up for her rights and puts the rights of others first (passive), or she comes on overly strong to establish her anger regarding relinquishment (aggressive).

Now you can give up this behavior because you have rights and you don't have to give explanations regarding the adoption , by saying things that you don't really feel anyway.

GIVING UP THE ROLE

Through the exercises in the previous chapter, you discovered and acknowledged the feelings that were repressed inside for so long -- and you also discovered the coping skills that were used to keep the system in balance, if only on a dysfunctional level.   Now it is important for you to find a way to change over to a more functional system of coping.   It is important for you to eventually (when you are ready) give up the role of the "False Self" as it is the role that keeps you from being spontaneous and happy a lot of the time.   It enabled you to pretend that you recovered and survived the ordeal.   The role was like a coat of armour because it stopped feelings from going in and from coming out much of the time.   Now it is time to remove the coat of armour and allow yourself to "feel" once again!

Much of the birth mother's spontaneity and inner instinctual feelings were repressed over the years. She often feels that she hasn't lived up to her internalized expectations. In many instances, she takes on an inner feeling of self-dislike. At this point, she feels a great deal of ambivalence because, at the time she gave up her baby, her inner feelings told her one thing, and yet she did the opposite by complying with authority. Much of the guilt that she felt inside was for having gone against her conscience, by listening to her "significant others".

As the years go by, the birth mother often feels a low-key anxiety of helplessness, isolation and inner conflict, but she tries to keep her feelings subdued in order to accommodate the shame. However, for many, this low-key anxiety can turn into resentment and anger towards the people who put her through the heartache years ago. **This anger can be directed towards her family, boyfriend , adoption agency ,or church official who sometimes told young women that as an "atoning sacrifice" they had to give up their babies. In this case "sex" was the sin and "relinquishment" was the punishment!!!! This outdated thinking has to be changed by those counseling young unwed mothers, because it is shame-based and humiliating.**

For some birth mothers, it isn't until they go through counseling that they are able to act out this inner conflict by counter-transfering their anger towards the therapist. You can also do this in a different form by using the Transference exercises that I gave you in the last chapter.

You can now begin to acknowledge the feelings, let out the emotions, and eventually give up the defense mechanisms by learning new coping skills.

We discovered that sometimes the "True Self" was buried inside the subconscious under pain, and humiliation, and the birth mother has a tendency to reject this side of the personality (we refer to it as the "Forgotten Self" in this instance). We also discovered how the "False Self" used defense mechanisms, as a facade, to hide the pain.

Now you may wonder just what is necessary to integrate the two sides of the personality -- to allow the "True Self" to be the dominant side once again. We will now explore the technique.

This chapter is about total awareness. You will begin to explore all your findings from your script therapy, sentence-completion work, meditation work, transference work and letter-writing work. The questions that follow will help you understand and explore fully to what extent you have suffered over the years.

Note: These questions should be answered after a few weeks of doing the exercises -- as this allows you time to work on the feelings and let out the emotions. There is no set time limit on recovery -- it is different for everyone, so take your time. Please remember that if the process is too much for you to handle on your own -- then you must seek out some professional help in the form of a proper therapist to guide you through your grief work!

1.   Have you suffered from any of the following
core issues of relinquishment over the year?

1.   Low self-esteem. (yes, no)
2.   Grieving the loss of your child (yes,no)
3.   Problems with   forgiving yourself and
     others involved in the relinquishment.
     (yes, no)
4.   Being out of touch with your feelings (yes
     no)
5.   Difficulty giving and receiving love (yes,
     no)
6.   Codependency (yes, no)
7.   Self-hatred. (yes, no)
8.   Dysfunctional sexual problems. (yes,no)

2.   Over the years, have you suffered for any compulsive behaviors to divert the hidden pain?

1.   Eating disorders (yes, no)
2.   Excessive smoking (yes, no)
3.   Shopping binges (yes, no)
4.   Yelling (yes, no)
5.   Excessive napping (yes,no)
6.   Excessive redecorating (yes, no)
7.   Excessive cleaning (yes, no)
8.   Excessive eating chocolate (yes,no)
9.   Excessive eating sweets (yes, no)

3.   Which, if any, of the following defense mechanisms have you used over the years?

1.   Repression (yes,no)
2.   Denial (yes,no)
3.   Projection (yes,no)
4.   Displacement (yes, no)

3.   (Continued)

5.   Avoidance (yes, no)
6.   Rationalization (yes, no)
7.   Sublimation (yes, no)
8.   Intellectualization (yes, no)
9.   Passive-aggressive behavior (yes, no)

4.   Which, if any, of the following illnesses have you suffered from over the years (possibly) due to stress?

1.   Asthma (yes,no)
2.   Allergies (yes, no)
3.   Skin problems (yes,no)
4.   Stomach problems (yes,no)
5.   Backache (yes,no)
6.   Unexplained aches and pains (yes,no)
7.   Sinus problems (yes,no)
8.   Anxiety (yes,no)
9.   Panic attacks (yes,no)
10. Chronic depression (yes,no)
11. Cancer (yes,no)

5.   Which, if any, of the following phobias have you suffered from over the years?

1.   Agoraphobia -- this is an absolute fear of certain objects or situations, making its victims housebound (yes,no)

2.   Claustrophobia   -   the fear of closed-in spaces (yes, no)

3.   Any other phobias (yes,no)

6.   The feelings that surfaced when doing your
script therapy, sentence-completion work, meditation work, transference work or letter-writing
work.

    1.   Anger (yes, no)
    2.   Shame (yes, no)
    3.   Remorse (yes, no)
    4.   Resentment (yes, no)
    5.   Guilt (yes, no)
    6.   Hurt (yes, no)
    7.   Loneliness (yes, no)
    8.   Numbness (yes, no)
    9.   Happiness (yes, no)

7.   The survival tactics that you used over the
years were:

    1.   Pretending (yes, no)
    2.   Numbing out (yes, no)
    3.   Avoidance (yes, no)
    4.   Denial (yes, no)

8.   Which substances, if any, did you use to mind-
alter in order to numb the pain over the years?

    1.   Alcohol (yes, no)
    2.   Anti-depressants (yes, no)
    3.   Tranquilizers (yes, no)
    4.   Other prescription drugs (yes, no)
    5.   Illegal drugs (yes, no)
    6.   Food (yes, no)

    Possibly, now you can begin to realize why it
was important to go through the exercises. You can
only work on a problem, when you know the full
extent of the problem.

The fifth stage of recovery is the "Bargaining". In this stage your empathy for other birth mothers has been awakened. Your awareness about birth mother issues is turned on and you can't stop talking about it. You will find yourself talking on the phone for hours to other birth mothers. Your feelings are really alert and you begin to become more aware of your senses. You are beginning to "feel" once more. [at least this is how most birth mothers feel when they reach this stage].

This stage is about bargaining with God or yourself. You make a deal -- that if only you can make it through the healing process, you will do whatever you can to help other women who have experienced the same thing. You become very sympathetic and compassionate to the cause. You may feel convinced that you can do a lot of sympathetic listening to other birth mothers. This stage is really about needing other people to validate your feelings as much as it is about validating other people's feelings.

I know that you may want to start helping other birth mothers right away, but I don't recommend beginning a support group of your own until you have a full understanding of the issues and conflicts that birth mothers have to endure. The reason for this is that many unexpected issues come up in these groups that you may not be quite prepared to handle yet. For instance, listening to too many other sad stories may have the effect of magnifying your own pain. When you run your own group, your phone rings constantly with other birth mothers needing to work through their own grief and you are expected to know how to help.

When adoptees are included in these groups, there is a chance that there may be some transference of feelings towards the birth mothers in the group. If you aren't ready for this, then it can really "floor" you. If you want to lead a group, it is important that you understand the core issues involved for birth mothers and adoptees, so that you can gain some control over these types of happenings with the group. Adoptees can carry a lot of anger in the "Awakening Stage", as can the birth mother, and sometimes the anger gets misplaced. This is exactly why this transference occurs. It is simply that the adoptees have different issues than the birth mothers. The reaction is probably on a subconscious level, and the adoptee doesn't always understand just what is happening.

An adoptee (who we will call Angie) called me occasionally when she was in the process of looking for her mother. It was a very frustrating search for her because she was one of six children taken from their mother at an early age. She was able to find the other five siblings, but the adoption agency, involved in the case, wouldn't give the family any identifying information about the birth mother. Angie would get quite angry with the insensitivity of the adoption agency, plus the fact that the search was costing her quite an enormous amount of money that she certainly couldn't afford. She also became quite annoyed at me because my husand I were in the midst of a huge search for our son and, on the other hand, she couldn't figure out why her mother didn't search for her six children. I understood that her anger was misplaced and it really had nothing to do with me.

The sixth stage of recovery is "Forgiveness" of yourself and others involved in the relinquishment.

When we talk about "forgiveness", in this sense, we aren't talking about a mushy sentimental process, but a heartfelt effort to try to let go of the old resentment and anger that you harbor inside for yourself and others from the past. Letting go of the resentment and anger allows the final flow of the frozen emotional energy from the subconscious. Once this forgiveness is acknowledged as being real, you are then filled with a positive-healing energy that propels you onward to a happier future.

Forgiveness is the beginning of accepting the past. It frees you from the crippling emotional wounds of the relinquishment. It allows you to let go of your unfinished business from the past so that it can no longer contaminate your future.

This blocked emotional energy can then be transformed into empowering energy, allowing you to live in the present and enabling you to create a new functional lifestyle.

Resentment causes you to "replay" old tapes over and over in the mind, giving the past memories more power to destroy your present and your future. Forgiveness, in this sense, gives you permission to let go of the past disappointments while you begin to dream some new dreams.

FORGIVENESS

Forgiveness isn't just the end product
of the healing process. It is the
beginning of a new future
in which you change your focus.
It allows you to move forward and
learn much more about life. It also
allows you to be more spontaneous.
You are a multi-faceted person and
now you are about to add more facets
so that you can shine more brilliantly.
You are about to become much more
than who you were in the past and who
you are in the present. You are limitless.
Your abilities are astounding.
When you consciously chose to heal the
past, you began the journey forward.
All that remains is up to you so go and
do it!

When you really delve into who you truly are you begin to realize that you are a multi-facated person.   You are so much more than just a victimized remnant of a past injustice, but somehow many birth mothers relate giving a child up for adoption as one of the most important aspects of their identity.

Once you forgive yourself and others and you let go of the locked-up emotions attached to the relinquishment -- then you begin to let go of a piece of your old identity.   You can then use your new attitudes and insights to mold a new image.

Through the recovery process, you generally take on a stronger sense of self-worth and you begin to focus more on all the good things that you are inside.

One thing that you should realize, is that -- had you not gone through the pain connected with the past   --   you wouldn't have developed other parts of your identity. For example, as I mentioned earlier, most birth mothers that I met during my interviews were among the most compassionate, empathetic and caring women that I have ever had the pleasure of meeting.   Had these same women not had to endure such pain and survived in spite of it, they may not have developed these qualities to such an extent.

When you forgive yourself and others, you allow yourself to give up the side of your identity that was hurting, and you let go of the resentments towards others. So, as a consequence, you cease to operate out of the "victim stage" any further.

Forgiveness doesn't just happen overnight. It may take much longer for one person than it would another. There is no time limit on this process, it is simply the end product of the on-going healing process in recovery. **In this process, you aren't asked to forget what happened years ago, because there was a lesson to be learned in what happened. That lesson was that being victimized is like having your soul raped. It is something that happened that can never be changed, but it changed your life forever.** Now you must take all the negative energy left inside (from the event) and try to turn it around to where you can turn it into "positive healing energy". Many of us do this by reaching out to help other birth mothers who are experiencing the same pain. When we help someone else, we also end up helping ourselves.

Towards the end of your recovery you may notice something peculiar happening. I have experienced it myself and I can testify to the fact that it actually does happen.

What I am eluding to here is that once you let go of all the blocked emotional energy from the subconscious, and you allow yourself to go through the forgiveness process -- then one day you wake up feeling a real sense of "love and acceptance" emerging from inside. It is sometimes so powerful that you don't know quite what to do with it. So what is this all about you may be wondering. Well -- I can only describe it as " UNCONDITIONAL LOVE". You are beginning to love yourself in spite of the past. This love also extends outward to other people who you may feel have hurt you. **You know that you are at the end of the healing process when this happens. At this point, the present has become stronger than the past -- so live in the moment and enjoy life when it happens!**

The final stage in recovery is "Transformation. As you transform, you heighten your awareness of what actually happened years ago. You begin to move from one level of consciousness to a higher level. This higher consciousness brings with it peace, empowerment and love. You also begin to feel that you have power over the feelings about the past, and although the situation back then can't be changed, your feelings about it can be.

As you transform yourself, you go through working on your core issues that were (in many cases) the dysfunctional part of your life. As these core issues are healed, then you allow yourself to become functional once more.

The transformation isn't easy, but as you learn to tell your story to your support group, close friend or counselor, you will begin to feel better about yourself as you finally let go of all the hidden pain.

You will learn to be more aware of your thoughts and actions as you develop your own monitoring system whereby you begin to pay more attention to your senses and reactions on various levels. Through all this, hopefully, you will never again ignore this crucial part of yourself.

Now that you have accepted the reality of how much hurt was buried inside, we will now go on to discover how you can begin to heal.

As you read the lists that you compiled, you are facing the reality of the situation. You have regressed and felt the feelings from years ago, and you have expressed the now "freed-up emotions", which hopefully released much of the blocked emotional energy in the subconscious. You should begin to feel more loveable, and open to new experiences as you move forward.

YOUR MIND IS THE TOOL TO RECOVERY

You trained your mind to hide the pain without having to fully acknowledge it. So now you have the chance to retrain the mind to heal itself.

Within your mind, there is an endless supply of intelligence and power. This power responds to your thoughts. As you change your thoughts about the past, you eventually empower yourself.

When you are so full of hurt on the inside, your mind tends to control you. But now, instead, you want to be in control of your mind. Your awareness about the old coping skills that you incorporated to hide the pain is heightened and you can now give yourself permission to finally let go of them.

Through your new self-awareness, you will be better able to monitor your own feelings and reactions to life in general. You can now distinguish what core issues still bother you, and you can continue to work on them. You are aware of any compulsive behaviors that you may have used to divert the pain, and you should now have the added incentive to want to change them because you are aware of the cause. There are twelve step programs available to help you recover from compulsive behaviors -- so if you are having difficulty in this area, then by all means, I hope you will consider joining one of these groups.

If you suffer from any type of phobia, and you are having difficulty with it, then you should seek out some professional counseling that can desensitize your fears. When you are ready, the ego defenses (or defense mechanisms) that the "False Self" used in an attempt to cope through all the pain can then be dropped as the pain is released, legitimized and validated. The survival tactics that you used over the years can eventually be dropped because you have survived the pain and have moved the healing process forward.

Finally, you can now begin to consider giving up any mind-altering substances that you may have used to numb the pain over the years. A bit of caution here though. If you are on prescription drugs from your doctor, then ask for his or her advice on the matter, because quitting "cold turkey" can bring on problems. If you are using drugs or alcohol to numb the pain, then it may be advisable to get help to give them up, because they have the effect of keeping your life in a dysfunctional pattern.

Being aware of your emotional responses means being able to monitor yourself so that you can change your reactions to things. For instance, you may not be consciously aware of when you are suffering from <u>anxiety.</u> The symptoms are: nervous bowel, sweating, frequent urge to urinate and/or quick breathing. If you find yourself going into the symptoms of anxiety, then try to relax by using deep breathing exercises, meditation or soft music to calm the mind. If the condition is prolonged, then be sure to contact your doctor.

<u>Depression</u> brings with it a different set of symptoms, such as slowing of the mental and physical processes. Many birth mothers can often suffer from <u>reactive</u> <u>depression</u> in which they becomes depressed when disturbing thoughts about the relinquishment of their babies come into consciousness awareness. However, sometimes the depression is caused by a <u>chemical</u> <u>imbalance</u> within the brain. Or you may suffer from <u>chronic</u> <u>depression</u> in which you feel depressed constantly to a varying degree. These conditions need a doctor's attention, so be sure to have this checked out, as you may need some medication or counseling to help you cope.

<u>Acute</u> <u>rage</u> can make you tremble and cause a rush of blood to the brain causing you to feel dizzy. You may also become physical and lash out to hit someone, or break a few dishes. Here again, you may also need some medication and counseling in order to get to the root of the problem, if this is a constant condition.

Women are taught to care for others more than or before themselves. It is thought to be selfish to care for yourself the same way you would someone else. We are expected to be understanding, affectionate, kind, helpful, reliable and gentle to others but we find it difficult to display these same qualities to ourselves. In reality, women are conditioned to center around the feelings and reactions of others, at the expense of experiencing their own feelings. You can see why the birth mother found it so easy to put everybody else's feelings first when struggling with the issue of what to do with her baby.

Self-nurturing is a major component of Recovery. Birth mothers must learn to nurture themselves, as it is a crucial area of power over one's self. Ways you can do this are: to learn to say "no" to others sometimes, and by doing something special, for no reason other than the fact that you feel you deserve it, and are worth it. Don't allow yourself to use any more negative put-downs about yourself. Tell yourself that **"YOU ARE SPECIAL!"** and keep telling yourself this.

Nurturing is one of the ways that you have of empowering yourself with positive energy. As you open up to nurturing and loving yourself, others begin to feel this energy also and it has a rippling affect. (Self-nurturing is really unconditional love for yourself).

Birth mothers, over the years, took a lot of criticism, both from within themselves and from others. Now you have to take on an inner protectiveness and compassion for yourself and don't allow any more criticism concerning what happened in the past. The past is gone and your survived it.

Once you have progressed through most of your recovery, it is important to develop a new focus. One of the ways you can change your focus is to use affirmations. Another way is to begin setting goals. When you have a goal, things begin to happen, and you are able to bring about change. Hopefully, going through recovery to this point has given you the motivation to want to take on some new attitudes and changes in your life. Once you clear out all the pain from the subconscious, then you have to change your focus and get busy with some new interests.

Through goals, you set out to make your dreams come true. Rather than just dreaming about life, "you begin to make it happen". Your focus takes on a new positive energy, and instead of reacting to things from the past, you begin to take charge of your life in the present. Goals, give us a sense of direction and moving forward, instead of the feeling that we are stuck in the past. They bring about enthusiasm and excitement when they begin to take shape and bring results. Goals often work on curing heartaches, because it takes your emotional and spiritual energy to accomplish them. After you have emptied out most of the hurt from your sub-conscious mind, it then becomes free to focus on accomplishing goals and moving your life forward.

Once they go through recovery, many birth mothers set a goal of having a reunion with their child. I believe this is the ultimate goal, and it can be a beautiful ending, to much of the pain. It is also the beginning of true happiness for many of us who have experienced it.

Goal setting is the central part of the healing process. All the other work up until this point has been preparatory. You may want to skip this stage once you have worked through all the other stages of recovery, but please realize that goals are "the wind beneath your wings" that helps you to create a new lifestyle -- allowing you to complete your healing journey.

RULES FOR SETTING NEW GOALS

1. Write your goals on paper and pin them on the wall where you can read them often. This helps you to stay focused.

2. Work on your goals one-day-at-a-time this way you won't become overwhelmed and want to give up.

3. Check off the goals that you reach and be sure to compliment yourself.

Two of the most important recovery behaviors that need to be incorporated into your recovery program are: <u>surrendering</u> <u>and</u> <u>letting go</u>.

Many of us surrender to a Higher Power (God) in recovery when we feel that we need a power greater than our own to pull us through all the emotional turmoil. The largest part of my own recovery was my surrendering because, without this step, I couldn't have made it through on my own. I believe that God, in His Infinite Wisdom, knows and understands our hurts, and loves us unconditionally in spite of them. When we ask for His guidance, He gives us the wisdom to pull ourselves forward through all the hurt from the past, and then He guides us into the future with a new added strength and love.

Sometimes we need His help to stay focused, because without this strong focus we have a tendency to want to back up the process and slip back into the hurting stage. When you operate out of that stage for so long, you are familiar with the feelings and it is easy to get stuck in it.It takes a lot of concentration and focus to move forward and find new coping skills to create a happy lifestyle.

Some of the birth mothers, that I interviewed spoke of being afraid of letting go of the past memories because this seemed like a betrayal to their relinquished child. To these women, it was the only part of the child that remained. But this is one of the thinking processes that has to be dispelled because the child is (possibly) an adult by now and is living a good life. You should believe this, until you have proof to the contrary. Think the best until you find out differently. This way you aren't worrying needlessly.

When we find these children, many times the thing that bothers them the most is the fact that the birth mother has had to suffer so much.

I know of one particular case where the son mentioned to the birth mother that he was carrying her guilt because of the way the entire thing affected her life. He "owned" the blame and guilt and this upset the birth mother, because that wasn't what she wanted. She just wanted him to know that she "cared so very much".

Letting go, in this instance, is to "forgive yourself and others"(for the part they played in having you relinquish your baby). In the recovery process you allowed yourself to let out the anger you felt for yourself and these significant others but, once the anger is out, **you are asked to TRY to forgive them, to finalize the process.** You can do this in person or by writing them a letter. The letter doesn't have to be mailed. The purpose is to just let the feelings out.

You have   to allow yourself to let go of the old hurt, resentment, anger, and sorrow from the past.   When you forgive yourself, you give up the need to punish yourself over and over.

Surrendering and letting go don't just happen. Methods have to be learned and then acted upon. The entire process   is about self-nuturing   and trust, and it takes a lot of work and conscientious effort.   But you can do it   -   just have faith in yourself!

Once the hurt has been uncovered and acknow-ledged and you have replayed the old memories, and let out the emotions --   then it is okay to let go of the hurt from the past.

Hopefully, you experienced the emotions in the regression exercises and physically and mentally let go of the pain.   Holding on to the past only hurt you.   The past is over and gone and it can't be changed.

Once the hurt and shame are released, you can then incorporate some new, positive coping skills. It is time to give up the compulsive behaviors and take on a healthier life-style.

Your need to hold on to the embarrassment, shame or humiliation should be diminished.   Also, hopefully, by now, you have received support from your adoption support group, a close friend or a counselor.   Your pain was validated as being real and it is no longer hidden --   it is out in the open, and recognized.

When you were carrying around all the pain inside, your "sense of self" was destroyed. Now that you are beginning to rediscover the "True Self", it is this "sense of self" that needs to be protected, as it is the part of you that makes you who you are.

You can now begin to redefine who you are and what you stand for. Learning how to give up the compulsions, anxieties and defense mechanisms takes a lot of self-discovery and inward work. Once this is accomplished, you must then begin to fill the void that is left once these negative traits are gone. You are now free to discover new opportunities and potentials that you didn't realize existed.

When you are able to give up the defense mechanisms that the "False Self" used to survive all the pain, and you learn to be kinder to the "Forgotten Self", then the two sides of the personality can be integrated into the "True Self".

This "True Self" now deserves a different set of rules to live by. Your new beliefs now become your foundation as you begin to create a new world for yourself.

When you are in charge of your life, your self-esteem, ego strength, self-respect and self-love become the foundation for being in charge of your life. Over the years, your belief system created the kind of world you lived in, so now you need to change your attitudes, feelings and thoughts about the world. If you are operating out of pain, then your world will be painful. On the other hand, if you are operating out of love and acceptance, then your world will be peaceful.

1. Be kinder to yourself by refusing to rerun the old hurtful memories over and over in your conscious mind.

2. Don't allow further put-downs about yourself.

3. Increase your self-esteem by reading books on the subject or attending workshops in your area.

4. If you are a codependent person, be sure to read Melody Beattie's books: Beyond Codependency and Codependent No More. (Harper & Row Publications).

5. Practice "total awareness" by handling problems as they arise instead of repressing them.

6. If you are still feeling shame-based, then I suggest that you read John Bradshaw's book entitled: "Healing The Shame That Binds You" (Bantam Books). Also, in many areas throughout Canada and the U.S. John Bradshaw can be seen on the PBS channel. (Tapes and videos are also available).

7. Learn the art of self-nurturing and use it to feel "special".

8. Incorporate some new goals and affirmations into your life to stay focused on the present.

9. Practice self-improvement. Try a new hair style, a new image, taking courses at college or university, etc.-- whatever works for you.

10. Learn to monitor your senses and pay more attention to your own "needs and wants" and allow yourself to do something about them.

11. Incorporate physical workouts into your daily routine.

12. Go on a reducing diet if necessary.

13. Change your focus from pain to thoughts about improving your health.

14. Give up your compulsions and replace them with a healthier lifestyle.

15. Allow yourself time to relax and to be play-full.

16. Take on a stronger sense of intimacy and love.

17. Reach out to help other birth mothers who are struggling through the grief process.

18. Celebrate your own uniqueness, rather than constantly comparing yourself to others.

19. Learn to manage your time better.

20. Ask for God's help when the going gets tough and you feel like you may back the healing process up again.

As the birth mother goes through recovery, and begins a search for her child -- the search isn't just for the child. It is also a search for the part of her that ceased to exist when the two were parted. In this journey she begins to see many opportunities and possibilities open to her that she wouldn't have believed possible in the past. It is a beautiful journey, and I believe that **William H. Murray** put it eloquently in the following quotation:

"Until one is committed, there is hesitancy, the chance to draw back, always ineffectiveness. Concerning all acts of initiative (and creation), there is one elementary truth, the ignorance of which kills countless ideas and splendid plans: that the moment one definitely commits oneself, then Providence moves too. All sorts of things occur to help one that would never otherwise have occurred. A whole stream of events issues from the decision, raising in one's favor all manner of unforeseen incidents and meetings and material assistance, which no man could have dreamed would have come his way."

I love it!!! This is what happens when you begin to search for your child. (I know because it happened to me). This journey is a " Spiritual Journey" because all sorts of things happen that you would never expect; and, sometimes it is by the sheer Grace of God that we find our children.

The path to regaining your own power is a struggle between your inner objectives: your mind keeps reminding you of the past, and yet with determination you are trying to move your life forward. Once you rid your mind of the "old tapes" from the past, you can set the groundwork for some positive thoughts and habits. One of the ways you can begin to retrain the mind is to use affirmations. These will help you to stay focused on recovery in the present.

A definition of an affirmation is:" a positive thought that we imagine, as if it were already happening in the present". If we say it often enough and with full meaning, our subconscious accepts it as if it is already true. You always state an affirmation positively. In your recovery work it is good to include affirmations each day.

You may feel a little uncomfortable at first -- using affirmations, but you must realize that once the subconscious is cleared of all the old emotional baggage, it is now time to fill the void with new messages. It takes time to set new patterns into action, so go easy on yourself and don't give up. Don't let whatever issues or problems arise set you back into hurting again (stay focused and on track!)

In order for affirmations to be successful they must have four qualities:

1.   **Present tense:** We state affirmations as if they are happening and already real. The subconscious registers feelings and emotions, so when we use the present tense, the subconscious accepts them as real.

2. **Meaning:**   Say or write them with meaning. When you do this you begin to internalize them.

3. **Emotional Energy:**   Affirmations must be said with <u>emotional</u> <u>energy</u> to give them power.   In order to feel the power, you must use your imagination to feel the strength within.   It isn't the words that count as much as the emotions that are connected with the words.

4. **Repetition:** In order to make these ideas a part of your belief pattern, you must <u>repeat</u> <u>them</u> out loud or write them at least ten times every day.

It takes at least thirty days to change a habit, so I would suggest that you use affirmations over this span of time to stay focused.   In a short time the mind begins to accept these affirmations as real and a new positive energy begins to re-place the negative energy from the mind set and feelings of years ago.   If they really work for you -- you'll want to keep on using them for the rest of your life.   Just change the affirmations to fit your current situation and circumstances as you grow.

<u>By</u> <u>working</u> <u>towards</u> <u>giving</u> <u>up</u> <u>the</u> <u>defense</u> <u>mechanisms</u> <u>and</u> <u>letting</u> <u>go</u> <u>of</u> <u>negative</u> <u>emotions,</u> <u>you</u> <u>have</u> <u>already</u> <u>made</u> <u>a</u> <u>positive</u> <u>statement.</u>   <u>The</u> <u>next</u> <u>step</u> <u>is</u> <u>to</u> <u>use</u> <u>goals</u> <u>and</u> <u>affirmations</u> <u>to</u> <u>keep</u> <u>you</u> <u>focused</u> <u>on</u> <u>the</u> <u>present</u> <u>and</u> <u>the</u> <u>future</u> <u>instead</u> <u>of</u> <u>the</u> <u>past.</u>

When doing affirmations, you use somewhat the same method that you use for meditation work. Choose a time of day when you won't be disturbed, then quiet your mind until you are in the Alpha Brain Wave State. You learned earlier that this is the state that exists just before you go to sleep when the mind is quieted down, and able to concentrate. At this point, you are open to positive suggestions. Next, visualize the new change as if it is already happening. Put emotional energy, conviction and feelings into your visualization. Feel the results, as if they are real and happening now. Make a habit of doing your affirmations at least once a day. The best time of day is usually early in the morning or before going to bed at night. However, choose your time according to your daily schedule, but be consistent and do them each day like clockwork. Say them out loud or write them at least ten times in a row. Finally feel your Higher Power giving you the strength to make the positive changes.

As you go through recovery, you begin to develop the courage to transcend what happened in the past and you will take on a new focus. In order to stay focused on what you want and where your life will take you, you need plenty of determination and dedication. In order to do this you must concentrate on your needs and allow yourself to be self-nurturing. Once you learn the technique, you will put more meaning into your life, and you will feel more dedicated to yourself.

The following affirmations are provided for your use. Choose a different one each day and say it or write it at least ten times in a row. It is also a good idea to make up some of your own, according to what YOU wish to accomplish.

AFFIRMATIONS

I now feel peace of mind and love instead
of anger and guilt.

I am one with my Higher Power, as I work on
healing all the pain within.

I am discovering with enthusiasm my True
Self once more.

The past no longer has power over me.
I am in control of the present.

I forgive myself and promise to pay
more attention to my innermost feelings.

I am now focusing on a healthier
happier life full of peace and love.

I give myself permission to let go of the
past as I move forward into the future.

I refuse to play any more negative tapes
from the past.

I deserve to be happy and feel loved.

When it comes to   proper counseling on birth
mother issues, you may find it best to go with a
**therapist who uses a <u>feminist</u> <u>approach.</u>   This will,
of course, be a woman counselor.**   This approach
takes into account the whole-person.   It considers
all aspects of the woman's existence and recognizes
the connection between her psychological and phys-
iological health.   It takes into consideration that
a woman's experience of reality differs   from a
man's view.   It is also a social change approach,
taking on a broader view of a historical develop-
ment of women, and believing that the present out-
look on things can be changed.

Quite a few birth mothers that I interviewed
spoke of seeing male therapists, whose .primary
treatment was the treatment of the symptoms, rather
than the problem.   They were often give mood-alter-
ing drugs as a routine   component of therapy, or
alone, without any insight as to how they should
heal the original pain.   In this case, the power of
the therapist to prescribe drugs is just not enough
to restore them to their full sense of power.   They
have developed their own way to numb the pain over
the years, and the last thing they need is to feed
into dependency.

Another issue to consider if you are thinking
of seeing a male therapist, is that some of them
tend to gravitate towards the psycho -sexual con-
tent of the past, and this has the effect of adding
to the birth mother's   quilt.   I mention this because many birth mothers suffer from dysfunctional
sexual problems.

It is sometimes just difficult for some birth mothers to work with male therapists; because, many of these therapists keep the woman locked into dependency on an authoritative figure. The message that she receives from such counseling is that if she just says the right thing to accommodate the therapist's belief system regarding adoption issues -- then she will be cured. This type of counseling doesn't allow for any new insight or empowerment, nor does it teach new coping skills to move her forward. It simply reinforces the fact that her feelings don't count, so she might as well just stop acting out, and stop resisting therapy. Here again is the original message that many young birth mothers received from everyone, back at the time of the relinquishment: "Be a nice girl and do as you are told". The birth mothers that received this type of counseling reported it to be of no benefit to them. As a matter of fact, it made them feel worse. Many therapists have difficulty dealing with birth mother's issues because of the old traditions within their own belief system. Traditionally, therapy has seen problems as lying within the individual woman, rather than in the influence that society had on the issue. It is the therapist's job to help the birth mother, because she is there for help. But, at the same time, the therapist has to understand that the social beliefs about adoption from years ago are not within the parameters of the world as it is today.

In recovery, the therapist must consider the different realities of both internal and external causes for relinquishment, because the birth mother carries the blame for everyone. It is important for the therapist to understand the external pressures

that functioned at the time to facilitate her re-
linquishing her baby. <u>She</u> <u>was</u> <u>made</u> <u>to</u> <u>feel</u> <u>guilty</u>
<u>for</u> <u>becoming</u> <u>pregnant</u> "<u>out</u> <u>of</u> <u>wedlock</u>" <u>and</u> <u>yet,</u> <u>on</u>
<u>the</u> <u>other</u> <u>hand,</u> <u>as</u> <u>the</u> <u>life</u> <u>began</u> <u>to</u> <u>form</u> <u>within</u>
<u>her,</u> <u>a</u> <u>spiritual</u> <u>bond</u> <u>developed</u> <u>between</u> <u>the</u> <u>mother</u>
<u>and</u> <u>baby.</u> <u>Now</u> <u>her</u> <u>focus</u> <u>changed</u> <u>because</u> <u>the</u> <u>issue</u>
<u>(to</u> <u>her)</u> <u>wasn't</u> <u>so</u> <u>much</u> <u>how</u> <u>she</u> <u>became</u> <u>pregnant</u> <u>as</u>
<u>much</u> <u>as</u> <u>the</u> <u>fact</u> <u>that</u> <u>she</u> <u>was</u> <u>becoming</u> <u>a</u> <u>mother.</u>
<u>This,</u> <u>for</u> <u>a</u> <u>woman,</u> <u>is</u> <u>the</u> <u>most</u> <u>wonderful</u> <u>feeling</u> <u>in</u>
<u>the</u> <u>world.</u> <u>Often</u> <u>through</u> <u>the</u> <u>entire</u> <u>process,</u> <u>no</u>
<u>one</u> <u>was</u> <u>realizing</u> <u>how</u> <u>she</u> <u>was</u> <u>feeling</u> <u>inside</u> <u>about</u>
<u>her</u> <u>child.</u> <u>Just</u> <u>as</u> <u>she</u> <u>was</u> <u>beginning</u> <u>to</u> <u>bond,</u> <u>she</u>
<u>had</u> <u>to</u> <u>put</u> <u>her</u> <u>feelings</u> <u>aside</u> <u>to</u> <u>appease</u> <u>everyone</u>
<u>else</u>. In counseling, the eventual aim of the ther-
apist should be to analyze and reconcile both the
internal feelings about her baby (that she felt at
the time of the relinquishment), and also the external influences that pushed her into making such
a decision, because they are linked inside every
birth mother by the internalization of the birth
mother stereotype (that she was a woman who simply
didn't care -- which just wasn't true!)

Typically, her dilemma results from the con-
fusion between her own inner feelings about having
to relinquish her baby and what society thought on
the issue. A major problem for the birth mother is
that she herself is likely to be the target for an-
tagonism, from both sources. Someone may criticize
her for what she had to do, so she in turn crit-
icizes herself. The birth mother may spend most of
her life sorting it all out. <u>Society</u> <u>punished</u> <u>her</u>
<u>for</u> <u>getting</u> <u>pregnant,</u> <u>but</u> <u>she</u> <u>punished</u> <u>herself</u> <u>for</u>
<u>giving</u> <u>up</u> <u>her</u> <u>child.</u>

In conclusion to this chapter I would like to mention a recent type of counseling that is being done on birth mothers. This treatment is to re-enact the scene by which the birth mother gives up the baby. The purpose of this exercise is to facilitate a proper "good-bye" to the child. I spoke to one birth mother that went through this treatment and she reported that it put her back into the trauma of years ago. She felt that this exercise really disturbed her. Consequently, she turned around and decided to say "hello" instead by finding her daughter. This proved, for her, to be the best therapy ever. She and her daughter have now developed a beautiful relationship in which they both are very happy.

[This book is meant to give you enough information to enable you to know the issues that need to be attended to, and to point you in the right direction for any further help that you need. Any therapy beyond this point, should be to build you up, rather than to keep you suspended in hurt or dependency.]

In all fairness to male therapist, I must add that some birth mothers have received proper counseling from some of them. I only write about problems that can occur for your awareness.

For many birth mothers, once the grief work is finished , they become anxious to begin a search for their child.   Some decide   to search while others don't.   Everyone's circumstances are different, so they decide according to the dictates of their own hearts, and sometimes their pocket books.

Some women feel that they don't have "the right" to search for their child. But, sometimes these kids are having a difficult time, and your presence may be welcomed and needed.If you are able to help with their education, this may be a nice gesture, as it helps the adoptive parents.

In many cases, adoptive parents today are often open-minded and receiving of you. I personally know of many beautiful   stories of reunions where both families become good friends. Sometimes the adoptee tries to integrate   or blend the two families together, but this doesn't always work well, because the adoptee begins to feel smothered. For this reason, it isn't a good idea. It is better to be respectful of the adoptive family and keep your relationship with your   son or daughter separate.   This makes it easier for everyone involved.   The adoptive parents deserve your respect and admiration, in many cases, for bringing this child up. Always consider their feelings.

Many of us go to support groups where we can get an enormous amount of information on the methods used to find these children. In these groups, we hear many stories of other reunions, both happy and sad, and we listen to these stories and share their excitement. But listening to others talk about their search and doing your own search are two different things altogether. As you get involved in your own search, it begins to take on a life of its own. It is like a roller coaster ride with many highs and lows. You will experience the ultimate in emotions as these searches are powerful, time-consuming, emotionally draining (but not as bad if you have gone through recovery) and sometimes (depending upon your methods) they can be very costly. But usually, it is worth it in the end.

The excitement of the search is like nothing else that I can describe. You become completely caught up in trying to find your child. You know that around the next corner may be a needed name and then you'll be on your way. You waited for years, and the time is drawing closer. You get to a point where you can't eat or sleep, and every waking moment is centered around searching. Everyone around you gets caught up in the excitement of the moment, and they begin to feed off your energy and enthusiasm. You feel that you are totally prepared for finding this child. But, let's explore what sometimes happens from the adoptee's point of view, when they are found.

When you show up in the adoptee's life, remember that although you are prepared for this -- your child   probably isn't, unless he or she has also been searching for you. Adoptees have issues that they are dealing with also, and sometimes when the birth mother shows up their first reactions is anger.   You must understand that this anger isn't just because you found him or her, but it is a type of "catharsis", such as the birth mother has when she first begins to open up her feelings from years ago. I know that you will relate to this.

Your appearance on the scene may bring a lot of emotions   out of the subconscious. Remember, anger is sometimes the strongest emotion, so it may have a tendency to surface first.   This anger may come across to you as rejection and, and it may make you want to give up, but don't! Hang in there! This part takes a lot of love and understanding. (I must add here, that many times there is absolute happiness from the beginning also, but I only add the possibility of anger to have you prepared in the event that this happens).

When you show up in your child's life, suddenly you are REALITY. For so many years, all he or she had to work with when it came to thoughts of you was fantasy.   It is sometimes confusing when you have to change fantasy into reality. The two now have to be integrated.

Within each adoptee there is a biological set of blueprints that predetermines many of their strengths and weaknesses. This is not to say that conditioning by the adoptive parents doesn't play an important role. However, when we raise our own natural children we find it easy to accept their failures and funny habits , because we sometimes remember going through the same thing ourselves, and we see a repeat of that pattern in our children. The adoptive parents, on the other hand, don't have the same frame of reference, so they may have a tendency to attribute these differences to the adoptee's failure to behave in the proper manner set out by them. This can begin to set up a pattern of expectations within the adoptee and they may have to take on <u>what psychologist call a</u> "<u>sub-self</u>" in order to accommodate what is expected of them. (This is very much like the system that the birth mother has had to incorporate within herself, to hide the pain of the relinquishment.) This may work for a number of years, but usually by the late teens the adoptee begins to rebel against this and feels some ambivalence within. For some reason, the issue of autonomy is stronger in the male adoptee than the female; and, this frequently raises the need for some counseling. The adoptee feels different within, because they have no biological reference to mirror-off.

Oh Really

Depending on just how much the adoptee operates out of parental expectations, they may become extra dependent on their adoptive parents, because they doesn't trust their own feelings. Too many expectations placed on them can have the effect of destroying their real feelings. This is somewhat like what happens to the birth mother -- when she was used to doing what everyone else expected of her,and she lost touch with her inner feelings and her natural instincts.

When adoptees lose touch with their feelings, their emotions can't always be relied upon and this causes them to have a disconnected sense of their own needs.

Under these circumstances, they may have a difficult time separating from the adoptive parents and even as an adult may depend upon permission from the adoptive parents in making decisions. You see adoptees have a tendency to be codependent also.

NOTE: This is not meant as a slam against the adoptive parents at all, this is just a problem that can happen, so I mention it only for your awareness.

When the adoptees are constantly expected to be perfect, they also expect everybody else to be perfect. The point that I am trying to make here is that, if adoptees have lived out of expectation most of their lives, they will put expectations on you also. You will be expected to be perfect --- just as others expected them to be perfect. Consequently, at first, your son or daughter may see you for everything that you aren't rather than for all the good things that you are. This is often difficult for the birthmother, but once your child realizes that your love is unconditional, then he or she usually relaxes and gives up on the expectations. Also, at first they may have you stereotyped, and this thinking has to be dispelled. Think of this as an adjustment period, and try not to let any of it upset you. You are just better able to handle the situation if you realize what is going on. What appears to be rejection, isn't really rejection at all. It is just that sometimes the adoptee isn't used to operating out of his or her gut feelings.

Many adoptees need to be told about adoptions in the past and the belief system that existed back then. They need to know that the birth mother wasn't a callous person who didn't care about her baby. They need to know that there wasn't a proper support system for unwed mothers (as there is today) and, in many cases, the birth mother was often treated inconsiderately by her family and society. She was shame-based and usually wasn't offered a choice. She was made to feel "bad" for wanting to keep her baby. She was told that the child should go to a family with two parents, who would provide well for the child, and give him or her a better life than she could provide.

In reality, we find out years later that these adoptive families had problems just like anyone else -- some of them also had divorces, unemployment, abuse etc. Just because they were screened, it didn't make them perfect. It was an emotional amputation for both the adoptee and the birth mother sometimes; because, often they both long to find each other, to fill the void within. It isn't natural for children to be separated from their mothers. This is why society is beginning to change its thinking on the matter. Consequently, many young mothers are keeping their babies with the proper support.

The process of getting to know each other takes time before any trust can be established. You almost have to be educated on the subject or you can get the wrong message from many things that happen in the beginning. And I bet you thought it was going to be easy --surprise!! Hopefully this book will have you prepared for just about anything.

When you are first developing a relationship with your son or daughter, it is difficult to know just what role you play. You are quite aware, that this person has another mother, but you are his or her mother also. A simple piece of paper, with a name change, can't change blood lines and genes. You may find that your maternal feelings for your son or daughter are very strong. The adoptee also has a hard time knowing how to act, and what to say or do at first. It is just a very special time for the two of you. When this came up in the relationship between us and our son, we told him that usually when children grow up and are out on their own, they develop a friendship-relationship with their parents. Our daughter has done this, and we suggested that our son do the same thing, if he wanted. We are well aware that he has another set of parents; but, when they are out on their own, they need to be validated for being themselves, rather than belonging to anyone.

There will be times, when you will want to buy your son or daughter everything in sight, and spoil them rotten, or you may want to give them money. Sometimes this is fine, but be forewarned, that many times the adoptive parents see this as you trying to buy the child's affection -- when this isn't what it is about at all. You just feel that you have a lot of catching up to do. It is sometimes confusing, as to know, exactly what do in this situation, but the best thing to do is to "play it by ear".

Another difficulty at first, is knowing where the boundaries lie. Who should initiate the calls? This is something that has to be decided, between the two of you. You don't want to be too anxious as this may turn him or her away, and yet, if you are working at a distance, you have to reach out and communicate in order to establish the relationship. It is best to learn to talk about your feelings as you go along. You will be able to sense if they need you in their lives or not. If they do, then you will be there for them, and if they don't, then you will have to bow out for awhile. I believe, that it is best to let the adoptee set the rules for this, as they didn't have a choice in the past, but **NOW** they do.

Sometimes the adoptee feels safer at a later point in time, to develop a relationship on a more mature basis. I know of one daughter that told her birth mother that she didn't have a place for her in her life right now, but maybe she would sometime down the road. This hurt the birth mother because she searched for five years to find the girl (finally having to hire a professional searcher). It didn't seem fair to her, in one sense, but sometimes the adoptee feels ambivalence if they are still living with the adoptive parents. They sometimes feel that they are betraying them. This, in essence, stops the adoptee from being spontaneous.

Although it is acceptable to tell your son or daughter about what happened at the time of the relinquishment, it isn't advisable to make it a regular topic of discussion. You aren't just a person from his or her past, but you are also a person in their present. I believe that it is important that he or she get to know you from a new reference point, of who you are today, and what you are all about.

When you first find your child, they may feel like a pawn for awhile, while they try to do a balancing act between the two families (this also depends upon their age and circumstances). They want to please everyone, but remember that their allegiance is with the adoptive parents, if they are still living at home. Once they move away from home, their life is their own and they have the power to make their own decisions. There is a lot of love to go around, and if the adoptive parents were good to the adoptee, then they shouldn't feel insecure about losing him or her. **Reunions should be about adding to -- rather than taking away anything.**

We discovered that the adoptee often feels anger on the inside regarding the adoption, and it is best to understand that they are justified in feeling this way. It is okay to let them express this to you as it also helps them to clear the air.

Another thing that can happen is -- if there was any abuse in the adoptive family toward the adoptee, often they may misplace the anger at the parents unto you for relinquishing , in the first place. Remember you are the safe person here and you must be understanding, simply listen and be nonjudgemental.

As these relationships are forming, usually over the first couple of years, you may reach a point when all these things spring up, out of the blue, and it may surprise you. This is okay, as it is about honesty. It is important to stay calm because this is usually a breakthrough point where the relationship can either become stronger or it can terminate for a spell. Be very cautions here!!!

This is really a point of emotional growth and love for the two of you, so let it happen. Once the issues have been faced, and dealt with, then the relationship usually has a stronger foundation from this point forward. Just about all the birth mothers that I interviewed (who have had a reunion) say they went through this stage in the relationship.

<u>The "honeymoon" of finding each other changes gears, at this point, and it begins to form a normal relationship</u> , <u>just like you have with your other children.</u>

THE ADOPTIVE PARENTS

It is wonderful when the adoptive parents are accepting of your presence. It is difficult for them sometimes but, I believe, that it is important that you are up front with them and honest. Sometimes they feel very insecure about you showing up. They aren't quite sure of your intentions. Make every effort to put them at ease. If they had a good relationship with the adoptee, this will never change. Actually, an interesting point to note here is that -- when the adoptive parents are receptive to the birth mother, then the relationship ship between them and the adoptee usually grows. It takes a lot of unselfish love and understanding on their part to comprehend the adoptee's need to know of his or her roots, as it gives them a much better sense of their own idenity. Many times they struggle with this idenity issue for years and meeting the birth mother often fills the gap. It helps them to become a whole person once fantasy turns into reality.

Many birth mothers speak of having a strong, spiritual bond with their child. Perhaps, it is because the original bond, that was established while still within the womb, was spiritual in nature. This spirit is familiar to her, for they knew each other's spirits. This is something far greater than the mere physical entities with which the adoption laws deal. It is a strange phenomena, but many birth mothers will tell of times when they had an awful feeling that something was the matter with their child (at a certain point in time over the years) and when she finds her child, she will find out that something actually did happen, at that time to the child.

On the other hand, many adoptees have reported having the same thing happening in reverse and they later found that something actually happened to the birth mother at the same time.

Another interesting thing that occurs, when you have your first reunion, is that you are better at sensing each other's feelings, then you are at communicating these actual feelings. What is yet unfamiliar in the physical sense, is better understood in a spiritual sense. I know that when our son came to visit us for the first time, there was a feeling of absolute peace and love within our home. We didn't have to say anything -- the feelings were just there and it was beautiful!! **Derek brought to us the feeling of completeness, and for this, WE ADORE HIM!!!** No family could have found a more wonderful son than we did. *Surely that's not overstatement.*

The underlining is such a nice touch.

Can a mother forget her

infant? Be without love

*If I was a male I guess
← ? I'd be a fruit to some.*

for the fruit of her womb?

Even should she forget."

I would not forget."

Isaiah 49:15

In my work as a Counselor and a Certified Graphologist, I use a tool called the Psychogram. This is a graph developed by Dr.K.G. Roman from her extensive studies in Graphology in Hungary. It has become a universal method of determining personality traits, used by graphologist today. It is defined as "a pictorially rendered profile in a circle" of the writer's personality projected in its entirety". It uses 40 indicators which exposes the writer's personality.

An over-all look at this graph, shows us the weak and the strong areas of the personality. It also indicates which parts are having difficulty and which parts are average or above average.

On the following pages, I will show you a case history of a birth mother and how losing her children 19 years ago, still has a profound affect on her personality today. This is presented for your general interest only.

In order that you will understand exactly what I am writing about, let's review the basic divisions of the Psychogram. Everything above the center of the circle represents the functions of the personality that have to do with our thinking, i.e., knowledge, philosophy, ideals, spirituality, and other attainable values. Below the center of the circle we find the indicators that are related to the material aspects of life, including the satisfaction of our various senses and needs, repressions, abilities, and fears connected with these basic senses.

Personality Evaluation Chart

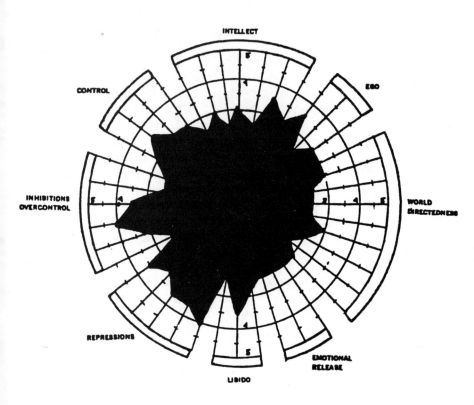

INTELLECT

EGO

CONTROL

WORLD DIRECTEDNESS

INHIBITIONS OVERCONTROL

REPRESSIONS

EMOTIONAL RELEASE

LIBIDO

Graphological Psychogram

The right side of the circle has to do with the extroverted side of the personality: how you get along with other people and society.

The left side of the circle has to do with your introverted side of the personality, the subconscious, and with the various ways you control your mind. It also shows your actions as an individual and as a member of society.

In order to figure out these scores, the graphologist has to measure 2000 different factors in the writing sample to figure out the 40 personality traits.

Now that I have given you a short explanation as to how the psychogram works, let's look at a case history of a birth mother we will call Jane.

Jane first came to me because she heard of my research on birth mothers. She felt that she has something to contribute to my study, so she allowed me to do a full analysis on her writing.

Sex: Female
Nationality: English/Canadian
Education: High School
Occupation: Store Clerk
Marital Status: Divorced
Medical Status: Under Doctor's Supervision
Hobbies: Pottery
Other Particulars: Lost 3 children to adoption

I first saw Jane in June of 1990; she was very upset by memories that seemed to be coming into conscious awareness regarding the adoption of her three children in 1973. She said that she had accepted what happened years ago and tried (without success), to subdue the feelings over the years. She thought she was handling it as well as could be expected, until recently when her mother died. At this point, she began to suffer from migraine headaches and general aches and pains in the body with no specific reason. Her general physician ruled out any virus and suggested that she go for some counseling. This led her to see a local Hypnotherapist , who used hypnosis to induce a trance, under which he gave her some post-hypnotic suggestions. One of the exercises that he had her use was to have her imagine that she was running a factory, and she was supposed to organize it the way she thought it should run (this was done in an attempt to help her reorganize her life). She discontinued the treatment after only six sessions because she felt that the therapist was only working on the symptom, and not the problem. It was at this point that she called me to see if I could suggest a better therapy that would incorporate her dealing with the adoption issues.

As we examine Jane's Psychogram, we notice that Jane has an average intellect, but her ego strength is low   due to her low self-esteem.   In the World Directedness sector -- it shows her to be more of an introvert than an extrovert.   Although she gets along with   others quite well, she   prefers to be alone.   In the Emotional Release sector, she hides her emotions   and doesn't let   them show.   In the Repressions Sector,   we see that she has a lot of repressed memories in the subconscious.   This is definitely due to losing her children. She is very inhibited because of these   repressions , and she has a   tendency to want   to fantasize about the children and life in general.[Remember we learned that the birth mother often internalizes the loss of her child.   This is a clear example of this.]

The Control Sector   tells us that she is allowing all this repressed material to control her life.

There is much more to these analyses that I am presenting here, (they are usually 30 pages long), but I am including this   chapter to   show you just how the   entire event of   years ago still has an affect on Jane's personality years later.

You previously learned how repressed memories carry pent-up energy with them. This energy is what I refer to as "negative energy" because it turns inward causing physical problems such as headaches, stomach aches and general aches and pains in the body. If you don't find a way to channel this energy and bring it out, then it keeps you feeling horrible on the inside. Because Jane's ego strength is so low, it is hard for her to come out of this situation on her own without some form of counseling.

She lost her three children in 1973 when her husband abandoned her. This caused her to have a mental breakdown and her children were placed in foster care. Since she didn't have anyone to help her when she returned from the hospital, the Social Services decided that it was in the best interests of the children to be placed up for adoption. Jane still isn't able to obtain any further information regarding the whereabouts of her children from the agency involved, even though it has been 19 years since this happened. They still refuse to help her locate the children because they feel that any involvement with the birth mother would upset the adoptive parents. This is sad because the children would probably like to know that their mother re-covered and she needs to see them.

Part of Jane's recovery was to let out the anger and remorse and acknowledge her true feelings -- the next part of her recovery was to help her to boost her self-esteem. She is now going through an extensive self-awareness program and has taken up a healthier lifestyle. Finding her children is the single most important thing in her life, so her focus along the way is to prepare for this wonder-ful event.

Epilogue

After reading this book, hopefully your consciousness has been raised regarding the lasting
affects that the adoption issue has on the birth
mother. Some adoptees and birth mothers, in many
cases, develop a sub-self (or fracture) in the personality, in order to survive the experience.
Along with this, you have become aware that there
is actually a spiritual bond established while the
child is still in the womb. (most birth mothers
would agree on this point) This connection remains
even though the two of you are parted, and it can
cause a longing, within each of you, to find each
other.

Therapists are becoming increasingly aware
that there is a deep need for counseling for many
adoptees and birth mothers. But, no amount of counseling can take away the need to find each other.
Maybe it is time that society began to look at this
issue, and realize that the biological maternal
bond is one of the strongest bonds that exists on
earth.

I believe, that the thinking about adoption
must be changed, and the human element needs to
be put back into it. Adoptive parents should
realize that the adoptee often feels a deep need
to find his or her biological family in order to
form a full idenity. Adopted children aren't just
mere chattels whose genes, personal traits and
blood lines can be changed forever through a
simple change in a name. This is something that can
never be changed, and to deny its' existence only
serves the purpose of keeping the adoptee locked in
a world of fantasy.

I believe, that adoptees should look for their roots if they feel the need. Sometimes what they find is good and sometimes it isn't; however,reality often helps to put things in their proper perspective. Maybe it is better to have made the connection rather than to have spent a lifetime wondering and fantasizing.

I,also believe, that birth mothers should do a search for their child if they feel the need; however, I would suggest waiting until the child is at least 18 years of age. Here again, what you find may be wonderful or it may be rejecting, but it is better to have searched and found out how your child is doing, than to have lived a lifetime never knowing and feeling all the pain. There is always a chance that they may need you in their life also.

Maybe we all need to change our old views on adoption to incorporate a new realization that blood ties are important. Wishing them away doesn't make it happen. Denial of the fact only delays the pain. I believe, that we all have this inate need to find someone who is a part of us. Sometimes both the adoptee and the birth mother feel like incomplete souls when this connection is severed. Maybe it is time that people (within the adoption movement) begin to wake up to the fact that the biological link is much more profound than they ever before imagined. The mental processes that we all have had to use to accommodate these archaic beliefs on adoption over the years is too devastating. It is time that we all reached out and connected with reality, and set out to find the missing link. As a birth mother, you will always realize that your child has another mother, but you are the biological mother who still carries the spiritual bond and blood line, and you must not lose touch with this fact. It is very important!!!!

We were fortunate enough to have found our son June 2, 1988. Finding Derek has helped to heal much of the pain, plus it has opened us up to love and compassion for others who have had to go through the same experience. Derek has added so much to our lives and we truely love him. He is a very handsome, sensitive young man. The relationship has had its ups and downs over the past four years, but the love is unconditional and we always seem to make it through whatever comes along.

For those of you who have read this book, I sincerely hope that it has been of some benefit to you. It isn't expected that every birth mother will relate to all the issues presented. But, I pray that it has increased your conscious awareness as to the depth of the suffering that some birth mothers have had to endure over the years, due to losing a child to adoption. I have experienced a lot of what I write about in this book, and it helped to bring about my own awareness that there really isn't much help out there for the birth mother. You almost have had to experience it to understand it. Hopefully, what I have written will be of some benefit to you and help you in your own healing process. When you begin to understand what is happening to you, then you can find a way to heal it. I wish you every success. If you feel that the book has been of some help to you and you wish to share your feelings, please drop me a line at the following address.

Heather Carlini
c/o Morning Side Publishing
P.O. Box 21071
Saanichton, R.P.O.
Saanichton, B.C.
V0S 1M0

Appendix

The following organizations may be of help to many adoptees and birth parents who wish to search for one another. This comprises a network of more than 400 search and support groups throughout Canada and the United States.

PARENT FINDERS
P.O. Box 3548
Main Post Office
Vancouver, B.C.
Canada V6B 3Y6

TRIAD (Society for Truth in Adoption)
Box 5114
Station A
Calgary, Alberta
Canada, T2H 1X1

AMERICAN ADOPTION CONGRESS
1000 Connecticut Ave. NW S-9
Washington, D.C. 20036
Assistance/Referral Hotline 1-800-274-OPEN

INTERNATIONAL SOUNDEX REUNION REGISTRY
P.O. Box 2312
Carson City, Nevada 89702

CONCERNED UNITED BIRTH PARENTS (CUB)
2000 Walker Street
Des Moines, Iowa 50317
Assistance 1-800-822-2777
or 1-515 263-9558

ORPHAN TRAIN HERITAGE SOCIETY
Rte. 4, Box 565
Springdale AR 72764

THE RESEARCHERS CLEARINGHOUSE
P.O. Box 22363
Fort Lauderdale FL 33335-2363

PEOPLE SEARCHING NEWS
P.O. Box 22611
Fort Lauderdale FL 33335.2611
Assistance/Referral Hotline 305 370-7100

Morning Side Publishing
P.O. Box 21071
Saanichton, R.P.O.
Saanichton, B.C.
V0S 1P0
604-652-6248

Please send ( ) copies of Birth Mother
Trauma @ 15.95

Shipping: please add $1.50 postage and
handling for the first book and $.50 for
each additional book.

Total amount of books ordered: ———
Please add shipping costs: ———
Total Amount $ ———

Check, Money Order, or Visa welcome.
American orders are payable in American
funds.

Customers from the U.S. pay no customs or
taxes on these books.

Visa Information:

Name:————————————————————

Address:————————————————————

————————————————————

Visa Number: ————————————

Expiry Date:————————————

Cardholder's signature:————————————

Note: Groups may request special discounts.

Do you wish to be placed on a mailing list
for information on other books available on
adoption issues in the future? Yes— No——